the

FRUSTRaTED

believer

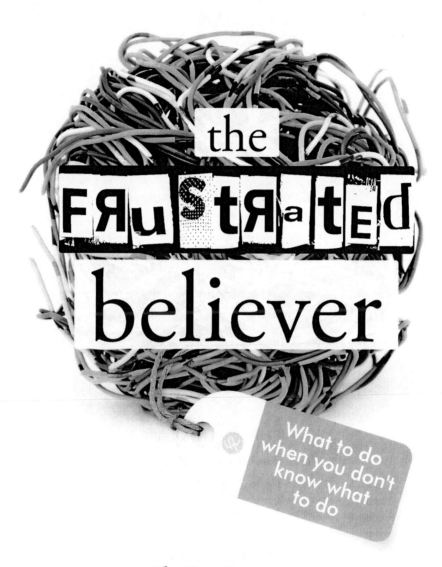

the FRuStRaTeD believer

What to do when you don't know what to do

Shelley Roxanne

Wilson Powell Publishing, LLC
Sunny Isles Beach, FL

Wilson Powell Publishing

This is dedicated to all my guys
Evan, Taylor, Myles, Jeff and T.L.
Your smile is my antidote.

With Gratitude

It is with sincere gratitude and thanks that I must first acknowledge the Most High God, who is able to do exceedingly, abundantly above all that I can ask, think or imagine. And for me, He sure has.

Thank you to my partner, my best friend, my boyfriend, my husband, Jeff for his courage to love Shelley Roxanne with his whole heart. I thank you, LuvaMan.

To my babies, Evan, Taylor and Myles for being my inspiration and my muses. Each of you blow me away at your sheer awesomeness. I learn from you guys every day. I live in constant awe. I adore you and look up to all three of you (literally and spiritually). I'm grateful.

To T.L., the first man I ever loved. You are the best Daddy a girl can ask for. To Glo, still Shelley Roxanne's biggest fan, your presence is felt every day. I feel you beaming with pride for your baby girl. Thank you both. I am forever grateful.

To my teachers, Dr. Bill Winston and Dr. A.R. Bernard. Your influence is apparent throughout this book. Thank you for your inspiration.

To the midwives who assisted me in various ways in getting this baby delivered - Robin Quinn, Jesus Cordero, Martha Bullen, Geoffrey Berwind, Sharon McKenna, Steve Harrison and the team at Bradley Communications. A sincere thanks goes out to each of you.

A special thanks goes to my dear friend, Crystal for your unending patience and support. I appreciate you. To my cousin Tillie, for standing in the gap for Glo. She and I both love and appreciate you for that.

To all my clients, partners and friends who have inspired me and had the courage to take this wild and crazy ride with me.

And finally, last but not least, to you, *the Frustrated Believer*. I know how you feel, I felt the same way, and this is what I found…The Best is Yet to Come.

CONTENTS

Preface

Normally, it's just the book's author who "speaks" in the Preface but this is a unique opportunity. In a twist, I'm also going to let my mother "Glo" speak through a letter she recently sent to me, and I offer that as the Preface to my book and as an answer to the question, "Who is Shelley Roxanne?"

You're probably wondering why this is unique. Well, my mother "Glo" transitioned eight years ago, so receiving a letter from her recently is nothing short of miraculous. But Glo was never one for being upstaged or left out of a good time so I shouldn't be surprised. Recently my father was going through a pile of papers at the house, and he came across a handwritten note addressed to me from my mother.

Keep in mind, this note —which he'd never seen before —appeared seemingly out of nowhere. Daddy had cleaned up this end table thousands of times over all these years and yet this note never surfaced until just recently. When he saw it, my dad was so overwhelmed with emotion that it took him days to send it to me. Thankfully, he finally did. Just in time.

The note reads as follows:

My Daughter Shelley,

You're the kind of person everybody likes to be around. You know who you are, and you testify to the power and principle of our people by the way you carry yourself. Your down-to-earth, fun-loving nature puts others at ease and warms up the atmosphere anywhere you go. I always thought you were a remarkable little girl, but you've grown into a dynamic leader who inspires others to believe in the power of being positive.

I love you.
Mom

Every time I read this note, which is now framed and sits on my nightstand, I cry, as I'm doing right now. It's not because I'm sad but because I'm grateful. I'm grateful that God blessed me with a mother who, even in her physical absence, is still giving me the greatest gifts a mother can give a child, which are unconditional love and unbridled encouragement.

Every time I think of Glo, I smile as I am enveloped by her shining, warm spirit. Glo was and still is Shelley Roxanne's biggest fan and, as fans go, she is as good as it gets. I firmly believe that special note, which had no date, was dropped into the natural world from the spirit world and came just when I, Glo's little girl, needed it most.

A great mother always seems to know exactly what her child needs, often without them asking, and provides it to her baby right on time. Glo is one of those great mothers. After receiving this encouragement from my mom, I am now refreshed and my purpose in life is renewed as I continue, as Glo said, "to inspire others to believe in the power of being positive."

Introduction

"Believe that you are here for a reason, get about finding out what that reason is and start doing it. Know that you not only have the ability to change your world, but you also have the duty to do it."
~ Shelley Roxanne, The Queen of Optimism

Dear Frustrated Believer,

There are times in our lives when destiny happens, when we meet exactly what we are looking for. I will go so far as to say today is that day for you. Your prayers have been heard. You hold in your hands the answers to the question we all ask at some point… What do I do now?

This book is a compilation of many years of research and lessons learned from my personal experiences, which were accompanied by much blood, sweat, and tears. Although many of the concepts may not seem new to you — especially to the person who has been on a journey of discovery for some time — I pray that this book finally sparks revelation for you. Because when revelation comes, your struggle is over.

If you are like me, you have been on a journey seeking purpose and meaning from your life. You have likely been bombarded by all of the gurus, teachers and preachers of philosophy and theology that believe they hold the very secrets to peace and happiness in your life. Well, it was not until I went on a treasure hunt to discover the truth for myself that all of my searching fell into place and made sense for me.

But first I had to look, really look, at myself and admit the truth. That truth was that I, although a believer, felt frustrated. I prayed, I followed the instructions of the gurus, teachers and preachers, and yet I did not see the results I desired. So, after the sudden passing of my mother, I went in search of answers. The very first thing I had to do was this… I had to change the way I looked at things. In doing that, I learned something very important. Spoiler alert… I will reveal one of the book's biggest concepts right now — It's not what it looks like.

In figuring out what to do when you don't know what to do… before anything else, you must change the way you look at your situation because it's not as it appears to be. If you learn nothing else from this book, I will give you the summary right here. As the great spiritual teacher

Wayne Dyer was most famous for saying was, "When you change the way you look at things, the things you look at change."

Know that the Power Lies Within

The primary reason for the frustration among those who are Believers is that we are looking for answers to the questions of life outside of ourselves. I will tell you right now, the answers are not outside of you, they are all contained within. Blaming "the Man," your mother, your father, your children, your husband, your wife, your ex, your boss, your employees, your co-workers or even God for the problems and challenges you experience is misplaced — and eventually this causes extreme frustration and despair.

And when prolonged frustration exists, you eventually lose your peace, and when you lose your peace, your health is not far behind. But, not to worry, together we are going to get to the root of this issue and get you back the faith, fire and focus you long for.

But first, we must awaken our spiritual natures. The power, all the power, lies within. Yes, the outer man must implement what the inner man directs but the focus and source is within. By misdirecting our own power, we are the ones who create the obstacles and problems for ourselves. I've got news for you; if you're continually having issues in your life... "iss-u". But here's the good news, if you're in crisis, that's great because crisis is good for you —it reveals the cracks. It tells you where you need to focus in order to be successful. There's purpose in your pain.

Revealing the Secrets

When my son Evan was about two years old, we had a conversation about Santa. It was Christmastime, and we were in the car. Evan was sitting in his car seat when he burst out with the statement, "Mommy, I get it, I finally get it." "You get what?" I asked him. He then said, "I get that Santa is real in the fake world but fake in the real world." At that very moment I knew this baby was far smarter than I was at that time. In his innocence and in his effort to try to figure things out —at two years old no less—he taught me something profound. Evan taught me that there were, in fact, two different worlds. One where nothing makes

sense and one where everything makes sense. The difficulty that we all have is trying to live successfully in both worlds, often confusing what goes where.

But there are laws, rules, even secrets, in each world to which we must abide. True, the frustration we often experience appears to come from dissatisfaction due to unresolved problems or unfulfilled needs. But the real cause of our frustration is simply because we do not know the secrets. In this book, I reveal the powerful life-changing secrets that you, the Frustrated Believer, need to know right now.

Being frustrated is not a bad sign; it's actually a great sign. It means that you are alive. You are finally sick and tired of being sick and tired. Contentment with things that are less than you desire them to be is no longer an option. You are destined (programmed) for greatness, and if you're not experiencing greatness, your spirit will not be content. The frustration we experience as believers is simply a sign to us that there is more for us, something better for us, greater joy awaiting us. We just need to make some adjustments to our approach (and our attitude). After all, it's all B.S. anyhow—right? (B.S. = Belief Systems)

You may find that many of these secrets you already know and perhaps have incorporated into your life but simply have to make small modifications. For it is small hinges that swing huge doors. But other secrets may surprise you as you may have never thought about it in this way before now. Either way, let this book be your guide, something you reference when you need to know what to do when you just don't know what to do. Or when you need reminding that you, my friend, are entitled to the best that this life has to offer —without painful toil for it.

Time to Awaken to Who You Are

Let's now lay the foundation of our time together. First off, your life is in your own hands. And it is perfect. You live exactly how you choose to live. Right now, you're living the life that you chose. You are a creator and have created everything that you are experiencing in your life. But is it really what you want?

That is the question. There is nothing good or bad about what you are experiencing. It's simply your perception that makes it so. But, if you want something to be different, you have the power right now to make

that change. But we cannot give expression to all the power within us until we awaken our spiritual natures and realize exactly who we are. We must awake and recognize the God within us. I promise that if you bring forth what is within you, what is within you will save you.

No matter your age, I highly recommend that you take the time to examine your life. The sooner, the better. Go back and revisit your accomplishments and perceived failures, and then draw the wisdom hidden in those treasure chests of experiences. This has been the most freeing and liberating — and the hardest — thing I have ever done. Giving birth to my children remains to be my biggest accomplishment, but giving birth to myself is an entirely different and rewarding trip.

For the past eight years — since the transition of my mother Glo — I have been in labor. It has been a process of rebirth of sorts. I'm convinced that when you lose your mother, the person who physically delivered you into this world, in order to move on with your life successfully after that you must be born again. It saddens me to see people who have lost a parent, especially their mother, who refuse to go through the rebirth "process". Instead, they labor with contractions and pain that they are not willing to address. Unfortunately this process, unlike the natural birth process, can be avoided — although this avoidance is not recommended.

Wisdom Learned & Earned
When I gave birth to my first son, I broke most of the blood vessels in my eyes. My eyes were literally bleeding from the inside. I must have looked like an alien to my newborn child. But I did what I had to do to get that baby out. I went through a very similar process spiritually in giving birth to myself. This book is the baby I delivered from enduring "the process." It came immediately following the rebirth of Shelley Roxanne.

As Jesus taught by parables, I will do the same here. I will share many stories —both personal ones and others that have impacted my life. While the messages may not be new, the messenger is. Although some are controversial, these basic truths are my truth, my whole truth and nothing but my truth… so help me, God.

Inspired by the great thought leaders of our time, on my journey of discovery, I received counsel and confirmation for what I already knew. That I myself had something to say that was unique and profound. I

xiv

couldn't hold it in any longer. As I turn the page to a new and exciting chapter of my life, I bring with me the wisdom learned and earned along the journey thus far.

"Finally I am coming to the conclusion that my highest ambition is to be what I already am."
~ Thomas Merton

Take What Works, Leave the Rest

I don't know about you, but mediocrity was never an option for me. I tried to live a "normal" life once. It was the worst two days of my life. I've got to live life large. My kids are large, my husband is large, and heck I am large too... and I wouldn't have it any other way. I've learned that it is living, really living (life my way) that takes courage. I'm now committed to go big or to go bigger, no matter what others think about it.

This book is not meant to preach to you. I sense that if you are, like I was, you've heard enough preaching. These are simply some secrets that I learned along the journey that I wish someone had shared with me long ago. Treat these principles as you would items in a grocery store. Take what works for you today and leave on the shelf what doesn't. But be sure to revisit the store at different points in your life when those secrets just might come in handy.

The Bible is believed by many — including me — to be the best and most useful self-help book ever written. According to the Guinness World Records, the Bible is the world's best-selling and most distributed book. It is estimated that more than 5 billion copies have been printed. Therefore, it seems fitting that it be used as a reference here. It is the guide upon which I draw inspiration and wisdom. While the Bible is the best-selling book of all time, it is also the most misunderstood. Keep in mind that the Bible is written to be interpreted in three ways — that is, figuratively, symbolically and literally. The problem that creates a lot of frustration is that people take literally what is meant to be figurative, figurative what is meant to be symbolic and vice versa. I hope to offer you another perspective to consider.

I am a shopper (a black belt shopper, I might add), and I like to buy my stuff wholesale when I can, so I go directly to the source. I suggest

you do the same. I will supply you with reference points so that you may search it up for yourself. Prove me.

My Travel Commentary for You

If I were traveling on a journey to unknown lands, I would take along my GPS. I would also seek the advice of people who have already gone where I am heading to get tips on where to go, what to do and certainly what to avoid on my journey.   As a recovered Frustrated Believer, this is my travel commentary for you as you go on your own journey.

But I have discovered that even with a GPS, there are no shortcuts to any place worth going. You've got to go through it – the good, the bad and the ugly. Be advised - once you enter "the process," there are no elevators; you've gotta take the stairs. You must do the work. But I can tell you that it is worth it all. In the end, you will hardly be able to wait for each new day to begin.

"I hope that my achievements in life shall be these — that I will have fought for what was right and fair, that I will have risked for that which mattered, and that I will have given help to those who were in need, that I will have left the earth a better place for what I've done and who I've been."
~ C. Hoppe

So I offer this writing as a love letter, part confessional, part instructional… on the powerful life-changing principles that now guide my large life. I pray it helps you along your journey to do life with a lot more fun, success, and chutzpah. Buckle up and enjoy your trip!

PART ONE

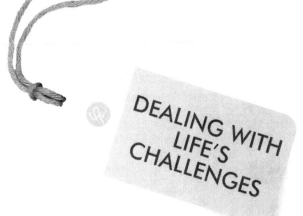

DEALING WITH LIFE'S CHALLENGES

Examine Your Own B.S.

"No one can create negativity or stress within you. Only you can do that by virtue of how you process your world."
~ Wayne W. Dyer

What's Up with Your B.S.?
You read it right...yes, I'm talking about your B.S. Your B.S. stands for "Belief Systems". (What did you think it was?)

You see, we process the world and the events of our lives based upon our belief system. Our beliefs shape our destiny. It is therefore very important that we examine those beliefs. We all live our life believing something. Even Atheists have B.S. The question is, is your B.S. working for you or is it limiting your life experience?

We interpret our world through the filter of our own B.S. If the interpreter is incorrect, the results are incorrect. The greatest source of frustration for most believers is that there is a glitch in their belief system. Your B.S. is unique to you and mine is unique to me. No two B.S. are alike. Something can happen to me, and that same event or circumstance can happen to you, but we may interpret its meaning differently simply because of how our B.S. has processed it.

To eradicate frustration, as in football, you have to shed the blockers stopping you from making forward progress. Let's tackle what is in the way of you getting into the end zone. And that begins with examining your B.S.

Your Thought Life
Since we know all problems exist only in our minds, let's go into the mind and figure out what's going on in there. It is written that you can

only be transformed if you renew your mind. Well, if you're frustrated, it's probably time for an upgrade in your thinking.

The Universe has a way of presenting to you exactly what you believe. If you have an unhealthy, broken belief system, it can destroy your life. Remember, the greatest self-help book ever written teaches that according to what you believe, it shall happen to you. It doesn't matter if what you believe is true or not, it is true to you. If you don't believe something to be true, no amount of secrets, proof or evidence will change your life experience. What you believe is what is being produced in your life. So, if you don't like what's showing up, check your B.S.

Contrary to popular belief, your circumstances don't make or break you. Instead, they expose you. They expose your true innermost thoughts. They let you and everyone else around you know exactly where you are. In what mental state you are residing.

How you react to life is very telling. Like a good email system, we too have an auto-responder. We automatically respond to life's circumstances based upon how our Belief System has been programmed. Observe how you respond to life's challenges. If you don't know where you are (in what mental state), you can quickly find out by observing your reactions to life. Then, if necessary, just re-program your B.S.

Examining your thought life is the most important aspect of change for a believer. Because to control your circumstances, you must control your thoughts. While we are instructed to think only on good things, that is not always easy.

Do you ever wonder why and how unwelcome thoughts come into our minds often out of the blue? They come from the "other" mind or the subconscious mind's previous exposure. It's like catching a cold. Somewhere, somehow you were exposed to someone with a 'cold' (wrong thinking), and you caught that 'cold'. The cold came upon you without your permission but with your allowance. That's why you must guard your heart. But we will get to that later.

Where Are You?
That's not a question about your physical location; it is a question of your state of mind. Where's your head right now? What "state" are you in?

Have you ever been to a theme park or a large shopping mall, and discovered that you are lost? The first thing you do is look for one of those large Directory signs that usually have a map on it with a big round dot that says, "You are Here." Looking at the map is key to determining your location. If you're trying to get somewhere different than where you are right now, you must first determine exactly where you are, in relation to where you want to be.

When Adam disobeyed his Creator, he hid. God asked him, "Adam, where are you?" While God certainly knew where Adam was physically located, he was really asking… Where is the Adam I created? The one who had dominion, the one who knew his power, the one with a strong awareness of self. That Adam. Not this one who has hidden in guilt, shame and condemnation for what he has done. Are you like Adam – beating yourself up over a past mistake? Get over it. Snap out of it.

You are not a victim. Drama does not just walk into your life of its own accord. Either you create it, invite it or associate with it. You are the creator. If you don't like the state of mind you're in, don't be ashamed or embarrassed – move. Your past mistakes are meant to guide you, not define you. Besides, the past is too heavy to schlep into your future, leave it there and move.

> *"To be a great champion you must believe you are the best.*
> *If you're not, pretend you are."*
> -Muhammad Ali

Free Yourself
You are self-imprisoned or self-freed. The first thing you must understand in this journey is the fact that "If it is to be, it is up to me. I AM the creator." No one else can free you from the self-imposed prison in which your own B.S. has placed you.

The keys to that prison are not in someone else's pocket; they are in yours. Stop blaming others. You will never transform until you own your own B.S. You're going to have to give up the limiting beliefs, fears and restrictions that are the weights that are binding you to your current state. You need to pack up and move.

Once you move to the new state, you must firmly establish yourself there. Lay down roots, buy new furniture, set up shop and lock the back door so that you don't ever return to your former state. You will know that you are rooted and grounded there in your new state when you no longer react to life the way you did before when in your former state. Now when life gives you attitude, you won't let it affect yours. You will have conquered the B.S. blockers.

As You Think... You Are

What are you conscious of being? Who do you think you are? The longer you are conscious of being broke, fat, unsuccessful, lonely, sad, etc., the longer you stay in that state. How do I move you ask? Simple. You can transform your life with this one realization... I AM the way. I and my Father are one.

Change the way you look at God, at yourself and know you are one and the same. One of the greatest questions ever asked was "Who do you say that I AM?" The Universe is responding to who you believe you are.

You are frustrated because the I AM (in you) is seeking to transcend the limits of your conception of yourself. To take you higher. The problem is you're looking in the wrong place. You're looking outside of yourself. But you won't find the answers there. Jesus said, "If a man says, look here or look there, believe him not – because the Kingdom of God is within you."

All that you desire is inside of you and within your control.

"For the truly faithful, no miracle is necessary.
For those who doubt, no miracle is sufficient."
~ Nancy Gibbs

Have No Doubt

The success or failure of everything in your life – your dreams, hopes, life, career, health and love – will happen to you directly to the degree to which you believe. A start to a better world, or a better life, or a better future is simply our belief that it's possible. Believe so strongly that life is worth living, without any doubt, and your belief will help you create that fact.

English preacher Frederick William Robertson is best known for saying, "To believe is to be happy; to doubt is to be wretched. To believe is to be strong. Doubt cramps energy. Belief is power. Only so far as a man believes strongly, mightily, can he act cheerfully or do anything that is worth the doing."

There is power and magic in believing. You must believe that something inside of you is greater than the circumstances outside of you — then you can achieve success. That is the true meaning of living an Optimistic Lifestyle. Live life believing.

Choose to Believe Again

If you believe your life is overwhelming and stressful, you're right. But if you believe that life holds unlimited possibilities for you, then you'd also be right. If you're praying but think that God is limited in answering your prayers, know this… God is not limited by what you're facing; God is limited by what you are believing.

Believe again. As a child before your B.S. was programmed incorrectly.

According to the dictionary, to believe is to have confidence in the truth, the existence or reliability of something, although without absolute proof that one is right in doing so. Only if one believes in something can one act purposefully. Your belief system is tied to your self-esteem. Not believing in yourself limits your world.

Remember, thinking is simply the processing of information. The way you think is just the way your mind processes information. When you get information, your mind takes that information and turns it into a belief. Then that belief affects your self-image, your self-esteem and what you believe about the world. Wrong thinking causes frustration. Poor thinking habits keep most people poor. Poverty is not a condition of your bank account; it is a condition of your mind. Because it is all based on how we "see" things.

We live in a cause and effect world. But what we are experiencing are the effects of something. That something is our thoughts. They are the cause. Therefore, if you are not pleased with the effects, go to the root

cause and change that. Then your effects (or experiences) will change.

Liberate Yourself

Have you noticed that people can lose weight on various diets, i.e. Weight Watchers, Jenny Craig, LA Weight Loss, etc.? But then some lose weight without being on any one of those diets. However, others cannot lose any weight no matter what diet they're on. It seems that anything will work if you believe it will, but the same works in reverse. Nothing will work if you don't believe it will. You create the experience you want by your belief system. The key is to decide consciously what it is you desire and then believe you can have it.

Have the courage to liberate yourself and let go of your limiting thoughts and beliefs. Such thoughts and beliefs are holding you back from enjoying your life's full expression.

We create our own possibilities and impossibilities by what we believe. When you truly believe something, it is unquestioned in your thinking. Your beliefs tell you what is possible.

> *"Miracles happen to those who believe in them."*
> ~ Bernhard Berenson

Embrace the Magic

If you're experiencing any level of frustration it means the Universe has shaken you to awaken you. Every next level of your life will demand a different you. You've got to grow up to go up. All that human beings have created throughout the ages shows that we as a people can do wondrous things. We've seen it in others. Our greatest challenge is to believe that about ourselves.

People don't seem to give their own B.S. the attention it deserves. Check yours and realize that the world is much more magical than you think.

It's Not What It Looks Like

"If you judge after appearances, you will
continue to be enslaved by the
evidence of your senses."
~ Neville Goddard

Life is full of "obstacle illusions"; don't fall for the fake. What looks like opposition is actually an opportunity. It's an opportunity for you to be creative. For you to rise higher in your consciousness. Sometimes it means seeing things in their larger context.

We tend to take things in our life out of context and then lose the greater perspective. This strategy often provides a great source of frustration. You see, we don't see things as they are; we see them as we are. We see the world through our lenses, which have limitations, lack and impossibility as filters.

Being the One that Bends

One of my favorite examples of this is from the movie *The Matrix*. By the way, that is typically not my type of film; I'm a straight comedy or "chick flick" kind of girl. Yet this classic movie has so many powerful scenes that are profound in many ways, that I often refer to it in my talks.

In one of my favorite scenes, Neo goes to visit The Oracle (for lack of a better description, let's call her a wise prophet who assists potentials along their journey of awakening). While in the waiting area he meets a little boy who also happens to be "a potential." Potentials were humans who had begun to reject the Matrix but perhaps were not yet fully awakened yet. Neo, while waiting for his meeting with The Oracle, watches the a young boy as it appears he is using some super powers to bend a spoon.

At first glance, he thinks that "Spoon Boy" is bending the spoon with his mind. Neo, believing at this point that he just might be "The One," picks up a spoon and attempts to bend it with his own mind. But Spoon Boy tells Neo to stop and recognize that there is no spoon to bend and that it is Neo himself who must do the bending. It is all an elaborate illusion.

Later on in the film, Neo confronts a situation that appears to be difficult, arguably impossible. He reminds himself that there is no spoon. The spoon is simply a metaphor for what we perceive as our "reality" or perhaps our impossibility.

This profound scene suggests that what we see is not actually what is real; it's only our perception of reality, and that is something we can change — or bend. We give the spoon, or reality, its frame, structure, and substance. We make it heavy or light, difficult or easy. It's all about what weight or importance we give to it.

I am reminded of that scene whenever confronted with situations that may "look" challenging, even impossible to overcome or solve, at the time. I remind myself that I should not try to change the situation because that would be impossible because the situation is not real. I realize it is me who is actually doing the bending. I am given the opportunity to turn the situation any way I want. It's never what it looks like.

You see, it's the looker — that's you and me — that needs to bend / modify. For we are to look not at what is seen — the circumstance or situation — for what is seen is temporary, bendable and subject to change. But we are to look at what is not seen — the truly powerful, enlightened You, which is unshakeable and eternal.

Never let what your eyes see determine what your heart believes. It's not what you look at that matters; it's what you see. Remember, it's all B.S. anyhow.

"Stop trying to change the world since it is only the mirror....
Leave the world alone and change your conceptions of yourself."
~ Neville Goddard

Living in Non-Reality

Another one of my favorite movies is *A Beautiful Mind*, based upon Sylvia Nasar's biography of the same name. I can watch that movie over and over again. It's based on the true life story of mathematician John Nash, a Noble Laureate in Economics.

The wildly talented Russell Crowe brilliantly portrayed John Forbes Nash Jr. in the film. While I understand that the movie's director took literary license with John Nash's true-life story, the film is masterful in helping us to look at our own lives in a new way.

John Nash, in the film, was a paranoid schizophrenic. But what fascinated me the most was that the three characters — his roommate Charles, the little girl Marcee and the Department of Defense agent Parcher; who travel around with John throughout his life and the movie —turn out not to be real after all. Because of his delusional hallucinations, John imagined these people to be real, as did movie watchers believe, until near the end of the movie. He had conversations with them, fights with them, held hands with them, had beers with them, and all the while, they were not real. Can you relate? I sure could.

One reason John's mind was so beautiful is that, despite his schizophrenia, he was brilliant enough to realize that these three characters never aged. John was a problem-solver, and he solved his own problem by changing the way he looked at his situation. In spite of his illness, he was the one, not the doctors who sought to treat him, who realized that what he was looking at was not reality at all. John had created those characters with his own mind, so he could deal with them with that same mind. It was not what it looked like.

How many times do we give our circumstance, that which appears real, all the focus and attention of something that is actually real? We don't have to be diagnosed as a paranoid schizophrenic to see something for what it is not.

Don't Drown in a Puddle

My husband Jeff is a tall, dark and handsome guy. He is athletic and has these big shoulders that appear capable of bearing the weight of the world upon them. My grandmother GiGi, always used to yell out

"Now that's a tall drink of water" every time she saw Jeff. One day when our son Evan was small, he Jeff and I went to a popular water park in Orlando Florida.

The three of us were frolicking in the shallow end of the kiddie pool, which periodically would produce small waves in the water designed to simulate the ocean. At one point, a wave came as we sat in the shallow end of the pool (less than 2 feet of water).

Jeff got knocked backward as he was not paying attention and did not anticipate the coming of the wave. He laid on his back, fighting and gasping for air. He was drowning. I watched him flailing his arms and waving, and I thought that he was joking, but I soon realized that he was not playing around. This 6 foot 5 inches of muscle was drowning in a kiddie pool of fewer than 2 feet of water when all he had to do was just sit up.

He didn't even have to stand up, just sit up.

We still laugh about that situation because he made a huge deal out of a puddle of water. It wasn't that serious. It didn't take a heroic event nor was he facing insurmountable odds, he didn't even have to stand to his feet to overcome this. All he had to do was sit up.

The waves were not real, the ocean was not real, he was a strong swimmer, but at the time it looked like this small situation could overtake him. How often in our lives do we misjudge the seriousness of a situation?

It is never what it looks like, it is a simulation, an illusion, and we are always more than capable of conquering it. Sit up and recognize it is not what it looks like.

Remember, the facts don't count. After all, you're the one bending, not the spoon. You can change the way you look at your circumstances, and your circumstances will change.

Life Is like Photography...
You Develop from the Negatives

"Problems are not stop signs, they're guidelines."
~ Robert H. Schuller

You don't go through experiences; you grow through experiences. Each and everything that happens to us is actually happening for us. God doesn't waste anything. Each and every event — whether perceived to be adverse or not — is either God-sent or God-used.

The stuff that we grow through, that we think, "Surely this is the worst thing that could happen to me" is here to make you better, not bitter. It's often in your darkest hour that you are being developed the most, eventually enjoying your greatest transformation.

Let Challenges Strengthen You
Our true selves are exposed by how we choose to react to life's challenges. When something seemingly adverse happens, you essentially have three choices. You can let it define you, you can let it destroy you, or you can let it strengthen you. It is your choice.

During these times, we are exposed, not just to the world, but to ourselves. Adversity introduces us to ourselves.

I saw an ad for an insurance company, and I loved the tagline. It said, "When adversity knocks at your door, won't it be surprised to find you have changed the locks."

Crisis causes you to reevaluate your priorities. Remember, all things work together for your good. Now while you're going through the situation, it's usually difficult to think that this seemingly negative situation is here for your good — but it is.

The best example of this would be Portia Nelson's autobiography,

There's a Hole in My Sidewalk: The Romance of Self-Discovery. It was written as a poem and done brilliantly in five short chapters. In her autobiography, Portia Nelson discusses how she experiences transformation while dealing with a challenge in life. I highly recommend you pick up this great book. In five short chapters, she takes us on a journey of blaming others, beating herself up, not taking responsibility, and then, by the final chapter, she changes the way she looks at the very same challenge, and somehow the challenge changes.

Lessons & Rewards from Wrong Moves

I was recently moved by hearing that the great Elie Wiesel, a Nobel Prize winner, had lost his personal savings, and his foundation had lost over $15 million in the Bernie Madoff scandal. But for Elie, the experience did not make him more pessimistic, nor desperate or skeptical. He said that beautiful things happened to him as a result of the American public's knowledge of his and his foundation's devastation and loss. Hundreds and hundreds of donations came flooding in from Jews and non-Jews, old and young, all over the country in a showing of support that uplifted him far greater than the situation had disappointed him.

My son Myles was telling me how he had actually learned to appreciate losing games because it was then that the team studied the tapes and analyzed what went wrong in order to learn from it. When the team won a game, on the other hand, they did not review tapes. How often in our lives do we do the same thing? It's only when things go wrong that we are forced into a form of reflection and introspection.

There seems to be no need to go through the exercise when things are going your way. I cannot remember a time when I was going through a difficult situation that I did not learn something valuable for the journey ahead. Now I make it a habit to talk to the situation (yes, I talk to situations), and I ask it, "What are you here to teach me?"

I've found that it's the higher expression of myself that is calling on me to come up to a higher level of consciousness. As soon as I get the lesson, the perceived problem dissolves because it no longer serves me. I have learned to be grateful for those times.

*"Souls are like athletes, that need opponents worthy of them,
if they are to be tried and extended and pushed to the full use of their powers,
and rewarded according to their capacity."*
~ Thomas Merton

Failure Made Michael Jordan Great

Most people believe Michael Jordan is the greatest basketball player ever to play the game. Few know however that Michael Jordan was overlooked back in high school when his coach was selecting members of the Varsity basketball team. Most would have considered that a failure, even Michael does. Jordan often talks about the 300 times he has missed a shot or the 26 times he was given the game winning shot and missed. Those are all perceived failures.

But Michael believes that it is those failures that allowed him to succeed. Would you see it that way? If you were cut from a team or missed important shots and lost games for the team, would you think you would eventually become perceived as the greatest to ever play the game?

Don't be afraid to make mistakes. Frankly, there are never really mistakes. They are just chances you took. It was another way to learn what doesn't work.

If you don't fall down, how are you going to know what getting up feels like? Failure need not be fatal. Perceived failures often turn out to be blessings dressed up in failure's clothes. Have you ever lost your job and, after some time, discovered it was a blessing because you were able to start that business or go back to school like you always wanted? But you wouldn't have done it if your job was not taken away from you. Sometimes through our failures we are forced into directions we ought to have found for ourselves anyway.

If You're Going through Hell, Keep Going

My father always used to tell me that suffering builds character. I would think, "Well, no wonder I have such great character!" I actually thought that I had suffered. Boy, was I wrong.

As an ambitious young girl, my big ideas, frequently dreamed up in Lucy Ricardo fashion, would often cause me to find myself in situations that I thought were challenging — at least at that time I did. After exhausting all other options, I would turn to my daddy. Most of the time, he would have a solution for me. Sometimes he would let me figure it out for myself. The older I got, the more he let me do that.

I used to be inclined to fight the situation, but I found the more I resisted it, the stronger it got. The resistance to the unpleasant situation was the root of the suffering. But over the years, I learned that the challenges I experienced in my life were mandatory to my growth and development. But the suffering was optional.

"Suffering has been stronger than all other teaching…
I have been bent and broken, but — I hope — into a better shape."
~ Charles Dickens' Estellas in, Great Expectations

My First Credit Card

I remember when I was in college, and I got my first credit card. Wow, I thought that this meant I had indeed arrived. I remember buying my first pair of boots. These leather boots were hunter green, with pointed toes and funky designs on them. They cost $329. I loved those boots.

Within a few weeks, I had shopped and shopped until the credit card got to its max of $2,500. I can remember this as if it were yesterday and how I felt when that bill came in the mail.

I got sweaty hands, my heart began to thump, and frankly I completely freaked out. You would've thought that it was a million dollars of debt (oh, that comes later, but I digress). I remember thinking at that time that the police were coming to get me.

Each time I heard a siren or saw a police car, I was convinced that they were looking for the girl who had run up her credit card to such an astronomical amount. You couldn't convince me that they weren't going to send me straight to jail, without passing GO.

Little did I know that the whole purpose of a credit card is that you get time to pay it off. I didn't know the police didn't care about confiscating my fabulous green boots that I had purchased with my new shiny credit card. To me, there was great danger in owing that much money on a credit card (a whole $2,500). I was terrified that surely they put people in jail for spending all that money on clothes and shoes.

As usual, I went to Dad for a bailout but to no avail. He let me work it out and of course over time I did. But it sure was scary at the time.

"In the middle of difficulty lies opportunity."
~ Albert Einstein

Outsmarting the Problem or Opponent
Thinking back on it, my dad was teaching me some great lessons. He taught me how to be a problem-solver. Such a skill is a lost art today. I try to teach my sons this very same skill. If you can become a problem-solver, you'll never be out of work. There are always problems to be solved, with a shortage of people who can successfully solve them.

So, if you are being confronted with problems, just consider it great practice. But don't fret. The problem always looks bigger than it really is. Sometimes you need to step back from the problem and look at it from another level. Besides, problems are never solved on the same level they were created. Again, you need to rise higher.

When you now look at the problem from a higher level, it doesn't look as big and insurmountable after all. Obstacles are simply opportunities to sharpen your skills. Think of it this way. The best way for an airplane to get off the ground is to have opposing winds coming against it. Like you, an airplane rises higher faster with opposing winds.

My son Myles is a talented football player. He is both a Running Back (offense) and a Linebacker (defense). He has the distinct opportunity to get a perspective from both sides of the field, depending upon which position he plays. It was my baby who taught me not to be concerned with the opposition because they are simply there to do their job.

Myles taught me that it is the job of the offense to get into the end zone, and it is the job of the defense to keep you from getting there. He showed me that there's no benefit in getting mad or frustrated at the defense because they make an interception or tackle you, which is what they are there for. They serve a valuable purpose. It then becomes all about your strategy to figure out how to outsmart the other side to get where you want to go.

Don't worry; the opposition is necessary for you to go higher. Embrace it.

"Obstacles don't have to stop you. If you run into a wall, don't turn around and give up. Figure out how to climb it, go through it, or work around it."
~ Michael Jordan

Life Is a School
Opportunity always follows difficulty, therefore behind every difficulty is an opportunity. People with winning attitudes focus on the end result (keep their eye on the prize), rather than focusing on the obstacles they may encounter to get to the end. Everything that happens in our lives is a lesson to be learned.

Life is a school, a constant state of learning. And just like in school, if you fail a lesson you must repeat it. Do you see yourself constantly struggling with the same issues over and over? Well, it's time to graduate, get the lesson that the situation is there to teach you, and move on. Therefore, you don't have to repeat the class.

As a mother of athletes who compete at the highest level, I have learned that involvement in sports does not build character, involvement in sports reveals character. I have seen such incredible resilience from Taylor with his swimming and Myles with football. They've blown me away with their ability to put things into proper perspective.

Without them having experienced challenges in their respective sports, although it was painful for me to witness, they would not know how strong and powerful they really are.

The adversity exposed their awesomeness. Myles told me that while the team measures success by (W)ins and (L)osses that he himself never loses. He said that on his personal scorecard, his W's stand for wins but his L's stand for lessons learned. It doesn't get any better than that.

If we changed the way we looked at storms in our lives and didn't begrudge them — but appreciated them for what we will become on the other side — perhaps the storms wouldn't last so long and be so frequent. We often spend so much time trying to get out of problems, instead of learning the lesson hidden inside the problem. If we focus on deciding what the problem is here to teach us, we will get better and not bitter speedily. This way, we can get back to enjoying our lives and fulfilling our purpose. Remember, God brings us into deep waters not to drown us but to cleanse us. Trust Him in everything, even the storms.

> *"The highest reward for a person's toil is not what they get for it*
> *but what they become by it."*
> ~ John Ruskin

In fact, it has been in my darkest hours that I have learned the most and gained the most from what would otherwise be perceived as a loss. Don't get me wrong; I don't welcome the dark hours. But I am often reminded that it is in the dark that some of the greatest things are developed.

Just like great photography and beautiful babies, you are developed in darkness. It is when you are in the valley that you can see both sides of the mountain, not from the top. Just don't stay there when you get down in a valley. Learn your lesson and come back up to the light. Better than ever.

If Things Go Wrong,
Don't Go with Them

"It is not a daily increase, but a daily decrease.
Hack away at the unessential."
~ Bruce Lee

If you're currently experiencing a challenge or even a crisis, it's important first to identify what you want, and then figure out what you're willing to do to get through it. Many times, your answers are sitting around you, but you are blinded by the problem.

Remember, you're working on becoming a fully skilled problem-solver. This way you'll never be out of work. After you get over your own problems (which should be quick), you can begin to help others find solutions to their problems.

There's a problem-solving process that begins with first determining what the real issue is. You need to begin with deconstructing the actual problem. Most of the time we focus on the symptoms, or the results of the problem, instead of going to its core. The solution is always within the problem.

Order in Problem-Solving
I used to love math when I was in college. My favorite type of math was algebra. If we were to look at a typical algebra equation like $4x + 6 = 14$, most people would call that a math "problem." That is where they first went wrong. The equation is not a problem. The only real problem here is the x. In this equation, we know the value of every other factor, so they are not the problem.

We know the 4, the 6 and the 14 to be unchanging factors. The only thing we don't know is x. So we go about deconstructing the equation by breaking it down to its simplest form. First, we subtract 6 from the 14 to get 8. Then we divide 8 by 4 to determine the value of x. Now we know that x equals 2. Once again, the solution is always hidden within the "problem."

For more complex math equations, there is something called the Order of Operations — also referred to as PMDAS. PMDAS is an order of operation in which you first solve the Parenthesis, and then Multiply, then Divide, then Add and finally Subtract. Of course, not all of your problems are math equations, but the point is that you need to have an order of operations for solving your problems.

Like with having an elephant as your dinner, you cannot eat it in one bite. Eat it one bite at a time, until you get to the core.

In other words, peel away at it, until you get to the core of the issue.

Learning What Needs Tending, What Doesn't
Frankly, the problem is not really the problem. Your attitude and approach are the problems.

The great teacher and writer Neville Goddard said this in his book *At Your Command*:

Just as a branch has no life except it be rooted in the vine, so likewise things have no life except you be conscious of them. Just as a branch withers and dies if the sap of the vine ceases to flow towards it, so do things in your world pass away if you take your attention from them, because your attention is the sap of life that keeps alive and sustains the things of your world....

So much frustration is caused by putting attention on the wrong things. You must turn your attention away from the things you don't want and turn it towards the things you desire in order to see them manifested in your life experience.

When you're undisturbed by a situation, it falls away of its own weight. Turn your attention away from difficulty and it will die. Neville suggests that you simply redirect your focus. This is not to encourage irresponsible behavior. If things need tending to, you must tend to them.

The key is to have the wisdom to know the difference between

what requires or deserves your attention, and what does not. However, it is imperative that you do not misconstrue something as a problem requiring your full energy and attention when it is not and does not.

The Constant Denominator —You

If you're constantly having issues, iss-u. You are the common denominator. Have you ever noticed in the midst of chaos and problems that there is the one constant always at the center of it all? It's you. If you want to experience something different, the change begins with you. If you're seeking more meaningful friendships, be a meaningful friend. We attract to us exactly what we are.

I have learned that God does not give us the people we want in our lives; he gives us the people we need in our lives at that particular time. The people in your life who irritate you are showing you who you really are.

If everyone you meet appears to be selfish and insecure, you may be looking in a mirror. This may be unpleasant to hear, but it's supposed to be unpleasant. It's necessary in order for you to experience your transformation.

Tubing on the "Lazy" River

Sometimes you just need to relax. Last summer, we went on a family vacation to the Caribbean to celebrate my son's birthday. We went on an excursion to what was supposed to be a ride through a "lazy" river. In this lazy river, you can either ride on a tube-like raft by yourself or get into one with another person. For some strange reason, against my better judgment, I agreed to get into a double, two-person raft with my husband, Jeff. Most people went in alone, but I agreed to get in one with him.

Now, neither of us are small people, so it actually took some maneuvering to get the both of us into this tube. But we eventually got in it. Hint: If you have to force it, it might not be a good idea.

As we were traveling along on what was supposed to be calm and enjoyable waters, we approached a raging waterfall. There was no way to escape it. You couldn't go around it, you had to go through it. At the same time, the waters began to get really rough underneath us, and the waves became intense.

My first instinct was to panic, and that's exactly what I did. Jeff was trying to hold me up at the same time that he was trying to steady the raft. That didn't work. The raft capsized right under the waterfall. The intensity of the waterfall and the waves of the water dumped me out of the tube. My head was banging against the rocks, and I was taking a lot of water into my lungs. I felt like I was drowning. Jeff was still trying to hold me, not realizing that I was right under the waterfall, which was moving like a raging tornado.

I felt myself fighting to get control.

All of a sudden, while still submerged under the water, I heard a still but powerful voice tell me to relax. That's all it said was... R-e-l-a-x.

I was compelled to listen. So I stopped fighting, stopped resisting, and went with the flow. I turned my attention away from the problem and relaxed right in the midst of all the chaos. Immediately, at that moment, my arm broke free from Jeff's hand, and I smoothly sailed through the water to a point in the river where I could stand up. I was covered with scrapes and cuts from the rocks and I was bleeding, but I was fine. I had on a hat, which surprisingly never came off during the entire ordeal. (Hey, I stay in style, even in crisis).

When Jeff finally got to me sitting on the side of the river, he thought that I was bleeding from my head. Red was dripping down my face. It looked like blood to him. But all it turned out to be was the red dye from my hat. It wasn't what it looked like. I was shaken but not stirred. For some reason I knew right away that there was a gift inside of that ordeal. I just had to open it.

"Only when it is dark enough can you see the stars."
~ Martin Luther King, Jr.

Looking at the Lessons
That experience taught me so many things. First, I immediately asked it, "What are you here to teach me?" Because I know that there are no such things as accidents or incidences without a greater benefit inside of them.

24

Everything, and I mean everything, happens for a reason and a purpose, and I know that all things work out for my good.

The sooner you figure out the reason and learn the lesson from it, the sooner you get to graduate to the next level. So I asked myself what I was supposed to learn from that situation. The first thing I did wrong was I had gone against my better judgment and didn't go into the tube alone. Or maybe I should have avoided the "lazy river" altogether.

Then the next thing I did wrong was I actually panicked at the sight of the waterfall directly in front of us. My panic was based upon what I perceived could happen to me... to us. It was my panic that caused me to get flipped out of the tube. Notice here that Jeff remained in the tube the entire time because he did not panic. He did end up with scrapes and cuts as well, but that was only because he was trying to save me — that is another lesson for another time.

My point is, my focus was misplaced. The other thing, perhaps the worst, that I did was once I was in the midst of the problem, I was fighting the problem. I fought the raging waters when I was in the midst of it. Bad idea.

The smartest thing that I did throughout that entire ordeal is I listened to the still voice that told me to simply relax.

Right there in the middle of the chaos, all I needed to do was to turn my attention away from the problem and relax. Only then and immediately then, in the midst of chaos, the exact same river that I was fighting was the very thing that carried me to safety.

The problem dissipated when I took my attention away from it and turned it towards peace. Even the great power of the raging river was incapable of consuming me because I stopped fighting it.

Soak It

*"People tend to complicate their own lives,
as if living weren't already complicated enough."*
~ Carlos Ruiz Zafón

Growing up in my house, complaining was not an option. This was not a home where you could sit around and whine about what wasn't going right in your life. On one side, I had my father constantly telling me that suffering builds character, and then, on the other hand, I had my mother, Glo, telling me to "soak it." They just weren't having it if I tried to complain.

A Mother's Wisdom in Two Words

No matter what problem you brought to my mother when we were kids, she would tell you to "soak it." Soak it? Are you kidding, lady? (While I was thinking that in my head, I wouldn't dare say it out loud.) I would tell her, "Mom, my leg hurts." She'd say, "Soak it." I'd grumble, "Mom, someone hurt my feelings." Again she'd say, "Soak it." Soak it was Glo's solution to all the things that ailed you. No matter what it was.

In her own way, my Mom taught me not to complain. Glo taught me to accept the things I could not change, to change the things I could change, to find the wisdom to know the difference, and to do it all without complaining. There was definitely "no crying in baseball" as far as she was concerned. I take the same approach now with my boys. No complaining is allowed.

I'm aware that this philosophy may appear insensitive, even cold, but it is not. It was the simplest most valuable thing she could have ever taught me, and I pass that wisdom on to my family and now to you. Looking back, her refusal to be an enabler forced me to put on my big girl

27

panties and snap out of it pretty quickly.

She wouldn't let me see myself as a victim who lacked control over my circumstances. This is probably what made me so optimistic.

Since whining wasn't an option in my house, I had to change the way I looked at things to find solutions pretty quickly. The fact is, everything has a solution, and according to my mother, a good soak could solve everything.

Stop Complaining & Pick Up the Mop

Make your home, your office, your school, your business, your car or anywhere that you are a complaint-free zone. Make it a point not to encourage complaints from those around you by perpetuating that behavior yourself. I have found no benefit to complaining. Resist the urge to even vent.

You're simply giving the situation more power. Glo always reminded me that if I fought for my limitations, I got to keep them. Instead of whining about what is not going your way, either change it or soak it.

If there's anything that I have learned for sure, it's that life is happening for us and not to us. I find that we tend to cast great shadows on small things. In the true scheme of life, most of the things we perceive as "big deals" are not really "big deals" after all. Still, let's face it... life does get messy. Things happen. But when your life gets messy, you usually have only two choices. You can cry over spilled milk, or you can grab a mop.

Complaining provides no benefit toward getting that milk cleaned up. The sooner you clean it up, the sooner it goes away. Complaining is simply a waste of time. Besides, what we often see as a problem turns out to be a blessing in the end. Look for the gift in your adversity, it's always there.

Once you know that all things work together for your good, you can confidently adopt the philosophy that no matter what it looks like, you can declare that all is well. Soon enough, those issues will lose their potency, and sure enough all will be well.

"What you're supposed to do when you don't like a thing is change it. If you can't change it, change the way you think about it. Don't complain."
~ Maya Angelou

The Power of Not Speaking Trouble

There is a misconception that optimists don't experience "bad days" or "hard times"; this is not true. Optimists simply recognize how important their words are. They know that they can give a situation life by giving words to it. Remember life and death are in the power of the tongue and those that love to talk will eat the fruit it produces. If you don't want more of what you're getting, don't give your words to it. Don't talk about it if it's not what you want.

My mother taught me such a valuable lesson about this. I made myself a promise that if I didn't have a solution, I couldn't speak the problem. Keep it to myself.

In an interesting and loving tribute, when Glo transitioned back in 2007, my girlfriend Marcia, who knew and loved Glo very much, sent me a gift basket of bath soaps, bath salts, scented gels and oils. The basket also contained a thoughtful hand-written note that read:

Dear Shelley, Soak it, Love you, Marcia.

Do Your Math

*"The hardest arithmetic to master
is that which enables us to count our blessings."*
~ Eric Hoffer

Count your blessings, especially when things are seemingly not going well. Do an inventory of all the good things you have in your life. You'll see how an attitude of gratitude will lift your spirits every time you feel down.

I've done this exercise when I felt overwhelmed or lacking in something. I did an inventory of what I had and what I was grateful for. It amazed me how much I discovered that I had when I shifted my focus away from what I thought I didn't have.

Gratitude is a magnet. The more grateful you are for the things you have, the more things come to you to be grateful for. A glad heart finds even more of what it's seeking. So add gladness to your gratitude and you'll be far on your way to realizing abundance.

There's so much to be grateful for if you just start counting. Start with breathing. I am grateful for breathing, for simply being alive. Start there and work your way up. You'll run out of words before you will run out of things to be grateful for. It all depends on what you choose to "see."

Gratitude & Happiness

Gratitude is probably the greatest key to happiness. If you're not grateful for what you have, you will not be happy — no matter how many blessings you have. I've seen multi-millionaires who appear to have it all, yet they are ungrateful. As a result, they experience depression, sickness

31

and pain (both physical and emotional).

On the other hand, I have seen folks who by most people's financial standards would be considered "poor," yet they are grateful for what little they do have. These individuals are vibrant and alive, and they experience pleasure in a way I don't always witness.

For instance, I met a man in Mexico a few years back. This man told me that he was the breadwinner in his family. His income was $250 per week. He supported a large extended family on that salary. He worked long hours serving and meeting the needs of guests at the five-star resort where I was staying.

I was struck by his indescribably magnificent smile. He exuded a peace and joy that I rarely see in anyone these days. I asked him about why he was so happy and joyful.

He began to point to the sun that was shining so brightly that day. He raised his hands and took a deep breath while tilting back his head as if to take in the sun's rays. He pointed to the blue water glistening below that sun, and he asked me, "What's not to love about all this? I'm truly grateful for all of it!"

Many people cut off any further blessings by being ungrateful and not acknowledging what has already been given to them. The soul that lives in thankful acknowledgment is closer to God than any other. If you remain and keep an attitude of gratitude and thankful praise, you will have a constant flow of good things coming your way. The grateful mind dwells upon the best. Therefore the best always comes to it. Develop the habit of gratitude so more can come to you.

"There are only two ways to live your life. One is as though nothing is a miracle. The other is as though everything is a miracle."
~ Albert Einstein

A Tourist in Your Own Town
Live like a tourist in your own hometown/city. If you don't happen to live by the ocean or in sunny Mexico like my friend, Jorge, you can still show gratitude for the place where you live. I'm quite sure, no matter

where you live, that people have traveled there to visit or vacation. Why not take a day or even more to live like a tourist in your own area?

Visit the Chamber of Commerce, a visitor's center, or a library, and read about the history of the place. Learn how the early settlers there gave the town its name. Visit the historical sites and take in the foods of the local vendors. Bring your camera and take pictures of things that you had not quite noticed before. You've probably passed by a monument or statue a thousand times but never really noticed it.

Having been born and raised in New York State, I can probably count on one hand the amount of people from there that I know who have visited the Empire State Building or have seen the Statue of Liberty up close. When I go to Manhattan, I'm always amazed at the amount of tourists — not just from other states but from other countries as well — who travel to New York just to appreciate all the beauty and magnificence that is there.

A New Yorker may go into the city and see traffic, congestion, dirt, poverty, and chaos while a tourist comes to the city and finds opulence, vibrancy, energy, richness, and beauty. It really is all based on how you "see" it. That's what living an optimistic lifestyle is all about. We are often surrounded by treasures that we take for granted while others travel from miles around to come to appreciate those very same things.

Living with a Grateful Heart

Once you make the decision to live with a grateful heart, you'll suddenly see things as if looking at them for the very first time. Each time one of my boys walks in a room, I am immediately awestruck with the beauty of who they are — inside and out.

I'm so grateful for their health, strength and pure awesomeness. I'm grateful that God chose me to mother these three incredibly beautiful individuals. Even when we disagree, I am grateful that they have the minds to debate and challenge what they think is right or fight for what they want.

Our thinking can be so different and yet I am blessed. As Jorge says, "What's not to love about all this?"

"We can only be said to be alive in those moments when our hearts are conscious of our treasures."
~ Thornton Wilder

In order to have an attitude of gratitude, we must change the way we look at things. Seek to find the gift wrapped up in every situation, circumstance or problem you are confronted with.

Living with a grateful heart also requires that you have a healthy self-esteem. To see the good in things, you must first believe you are worthy of good. I often talk about the identity crisis that I am convinced that modern-day people all over the world suffer from.

If you truly understood how beautifully, wonderfully and masterfully you were made, and if you truly knew just how precious you are, you would find it a lot easier to find the good in things because you'd know you deserve it.

Unwrapping the Gifts in Adversity

To find the good to be grateful for, I often dissect an adversity as if it were an insect. I look at it from every angle, and sometimes it needs a microscope. But the silver lining is always there, often hidden from sight when looking at it with your eyes but very apparent when you're looking at it with your heart.

When life gets messy for this optimist, I find myself immediately going to gratitude as the default. I'm reminded that all things work together for my good. I'm reminded that this too shall pass.

Yes, at those challenging times, I'm reminded that this situation has been presented as a gift for me, and it's my job to go about the process of unwrapping it. Once you see life and everything in it as a gift, it's very simple to be grateful.

I mean who doesn't love getting gifts?

And the Gifts Keep Coming

Each day when you awake up, you're given the gift of living that day, and then throughout the day, the gifts keep on coming. No matter who you are, you have so much to be grateful for. Start counting.

Nobody Puts Baby
in a Corner

"Don't be distracted by criticism. Remember,
the only taste of success some people have is
when they take a bite out of you."
~ Zig Ziglar

Only Baby can put Baby in a corner. No one else is even capable of doing it. It's no one's fault for where you are in your life. We are all exactly where we want to be. No one can do anything to you without your permission. You see, we're only confined by the walls we build for ourselves.

The keys to your happiness are not in someone else's pocket; they are in yours.

Resist the urge to play the blame game. It is a failed attempt to take the responsibility off of ourselves and falsely put it on others. Martin Luther King, Jr. once said, "A man can't ride your back unless it is bent." We're supposed to stand up for ourselves and take full responsibility for what is happening in our own lives. So often, I lamented about why people were riding me and why I was not getting out of the relationship what I needed. Then I realized that it was not up to them; it was up to me.

I just needed to stand up... to declare what I wanted and needed out of the relationship. If they were unwilling to give it, then I was unwilling to accept less. Frankly, you are the light of the world. Don't let someone dim your light simply because it's shining in their eyes. Let your light so shine.

Conviction in the Midst of Controversy

When you begin this journey of striving for more and better in your life, get ready to lose some friends and be criticized. Let's face it; it takes courage to hold your conviction in the midst of controversy. That's what Martin Luther King, Jr. said was the ultimate test of a person. Not where they stand in times of comfort and convenience, but where they stand in times of challenge and controversy.

This is the true test of a person. Hey, it's easy to be upbeat and nice when things are going your way. But how do you act when your back is up against a wall? Do you run at the first sign of trouble or do you stand tall and hold your ground? Have you ever had an unpopular view or opinion but failed to express it because your friends and family may not approve or wouldn't agree?

Often, you're given a vision or idea, and it is yours and yours alone. It was not given to your spouse or to your best friend; it was given to you. If you held back on addressing that because the people around you may not approve, you were not doing your job of fulfilling your life's purpose.

Make a list of the things you have decided to tolerate no longer in your life. Stick to the list no matter what. Know that these things are directly tied to your self-esteem. You only put up with certain things because you deep down believe you deserve it. No one, and I mean no one, can stop you from reaching your destiny but you.

Raise your own sense of self-worth, and you will certainly see things turn around for you. Fewer people will be trying to put Baby in a corner because Baby won't have it anymore.

"You have to learn to get up from the table when love is no longer being served."
- Nina Simone

Stand Up for Yourself
I realize we all want to belong to something, which is why we should teach our children the importance of family and a strong self-esteem. No one wants to feel like an outsider and standing up to a bully is not easy for anyone at any age. This is another conversation I have continually with my sons.

A good healthy self-image is important because all of the choices you make come out of that self-image. We tend to hang out with people because somehow, someway, they provide some benefits to us for doing so. I remember as a young girl, I spent a lot of time with people simply because they liked me. Now don't get me wrong, that is not a bad thing.

The problem was that I didn't like them very much. The fact that they liked me was simply evidence of their good taste. I know that now, the problem is I didn't know it then.

But I was not strong enough in my self-esteem at that time to stand-up for my own good taste. In fairness, they were not terrible people. They were just not authentic people. Although they were perhaps nice to me, these people were not very nice to others. I did not like where they were going and didn't want to go there. Even though I spent time with these people socially, even as a young girl, I did not fall prey to peer pressure. The reality is that I didn't drink when everyone else was drinking, and I didn't smoke when everyone else was smoking.

I respected myself better than that but still I let people into my life that were not qualified to be there, all because I was not willing to walk alone. The more that I liked myself and the quality of my own company, the more I was willing to cut people off who did not properly reflect who I was as a person. That is when I decided that I should re-evaluate my relationships. I call it pruning.

To prune means to cut off or eliminate anything superfluous or undesirable. I go through a pruning process every so often regarding my relationships with people and projects in my life. After some time, I evaluate whether the relationship or project is producing fruit. If it is not, I have to cut it off. It is a necessary process that we all must go through. It allows the good stuff to flourish and grow better because you pruned the weeds and twigs.

It is a painful process – Yes. Can it be lonely – Yes. It is the best thing you can do for yourself – Yes. I learned, through maturity, of course, to enjoy my own company and not to allow people in my life who did not deserve to be there. Regardless of whether they would be mad at me or not for demanding more for myself.

Who Are You Attracting into Your Life?
This may be a more difficult principles to follow because we are all social creatures and love being around people. We love being popular and well-liked, and some will do just about anything for that attention.

Now I'm not suggesting you become a recluse. I am however

suggesting that you be keenly aware of your surroundings and decide if your current group of friends represent who you are or who you want to be. Simply recognize that when in the developmental stages of your life, it is important not to pick up habits that belong to someone else.

You will quickly learn that as you move up to higher levels in life, you will have and need less and less friends. The good news is that the relationships with the ones left standing are much stronger, richer and more meaningful. But again, you must first be an authentic friend if you want to have authentic friends.

You attract exactly what you are. If you don't like the people you are currently attracting, change the attractor.

Maturity & Wisdom

Attracting authentic friends is also one of the great benefits of growing in maturity. Contrary to popular belief, maturity is not an expression of age. True maturity is the acceptance of responsibility. I know some very mature people who are quite young, just as I know far too many immature people who are a lot older. So age has very little to do with maturity, although perhaps it should. With age comes experience or at least time spent living.

I like to give people who have lived longer the benefit of the doubt that they might have learned some things over the years. Some of the most valuable things I have learned in my life have come when I have taken the time to sit at the feet of my elders and just listen to their wisdom. I am someone who doesn't like to waste a lot of time. So if I can learn from someone who has wisdom and experience, I will invest the time to gain that information by hanging out with them.

Be Gentle with Yourself While Becoming Your Best

Teach people how to treat you by being gentle with yourself. Forgive and forget easily. R.S.V.P. - Not Attending - to all pity party invitations. You are not a victim; you are a victor. Your friends are like mirrors, simply reflecting back to you exactly what you're giving yourself.

Your reflection is seen in the eyes of your friends. We tend to attract who we are. Yet we are attracted to those we want to be. The greatest thing you can do for your friends and the world is to make the most of yourself.

Everybody Plays the Fool Sometimes

*"Accept that some days you're the pigeon and
some days you're the statue."*
~ Thomas Merton

We will get fooled by people. That's OK. If you learned something from the experience, it was not a waste of time. Education always costs you something. But there is a simple secret to determining who is who in your life. Follow the philosophy that a tree is recognized by its fruit and you will be fine.

Does the Telling & Showing Match?

Once again, a tree is recognized or identified by the fruit it produces. If you want to truly know someone, examine the fruit produced in their lives. If they are telling you one thing and showing you something very different, this would be one of those rare times when you must believe what you see.

Frankly, if you were told that this is an apple tree, but all you see in front of you are oranges hanging from it, it is safe to assume it is not an apple tree.

Today people are so skilled at presenting a front. It's often difficult to determine who and what is true and who and what is false. But it's not that difficult if we open our eyes — the spiritual ones.

If you have the eyes to see and the ears to hear, you will always know what you're dealing with.

Our Lives as Movies

Your entire life is a movie for which you are the director, producer, writer and lead actor. The people in your life are actors who co-star with you in your movie. To examine this further, let's look at the part characters play in actual movies.

In your favorite film, the characters in the movie can be dynamic characters with complexity and depth — but this depends upon the writer's intention and purpose for each character. In movies, some characters are main characters who appear in the entire film, while others appear only in certain scenes. There are always tons of extras who are clearly there for the purpose of creating a certain environment for the rest of the film to play itself out.

Our lives are just the same. You will find that there are people in your life who are main characters; they will stay with you the entire way through. This is not necessarily solely in the physical sense, but their presence is felt throughout your entire life story. Then there are people who may only be in your life for a particular season.

Maybe it is a childhood friend, and when you were younger, the two of you were inseparable. Somehow you grew apart. That is OK. They were meant to be there in your movie only for particular scenes (seasons). Then there are the people who are in your life perhaps for just a moment — but for a very specific reason. You want to pay particular attention to them.

Have you ever watched a mystery movie? With mysteries, it is our job as the viewer to figure out or solve a particular who-done-it. The director will always help us out by revealing certain secrets to give us hints and clues along the way. So it is with your life. As the director, when you planned out this life of yours, you pre-designed it with clues as to the who, what, when, where and how of the mysteries in your life. As they unfold, it is now your job as the main character to play out the scenes and to pay attention to the clues to discover the meaning and moral of your story.

There are some important keys here. First, never try to force an extra to become a main character. They are meant to be in the background; leave them there. Second, don't ignore the clues given you by the people who are there for a reason. When people tell you important information, by showing you who they are, believe them. They're trying to tell you something crucial. Accept it and move on, whether you like what they're telling you or not.

And finally, never disrespect the people who are in your movie (life) for the duration. These people are in it for the long haul, and you designed it that way. Reward them with your love, respect, and attention. Appreciate them for the significance that they bring to your life's journey. They are the only ones truly eligible for your academy's award.

Failure & Success
You may need to kiss a few frogs to find your prince or princess. And you may make some mistakes in opening up and getting close to certain friends and family members. But failure is the condiment that gives success its flavor.

Once you find your true loves (this includes friends, lovers, and favorite family members), you will recognize them and appreciate them more.

PART TWO

RELATIONSHIP
WITH
SELF

Smash Your Give-a-Damner

"I will not let anyone walk through my mind
with their dirty feet."
~ Mahatma Gandhi

Oh, I really love this one. If you truly want to get your power back, you must take a hammer, a really huge one, and take a whack at your "Give-a-Damner."

Right off the bat, let's get something straight. A Give-a-Damner is a sort of device (symbolic, not literal) which is powered by the ego. It's the thing that stops you from taking risks in life. It's the thing that stops you from fully being you. It's the thing that eventually suffocates your dreams. It's an evil thing, and you have to break it. Take out its batteries.

Do whatever you have to do to make that thing stop working.

Life without a Give-a-Damner

When your Give-a-Damner is broken, it doesn't mean that you don't care about people. It simply means that you care less and less about what people think or say about you.

When your Give-a-Damner is broken, you shine in every situation and have the courage to be you no matter what others think. You live in a freedom that few people ever experience. You are liberated from the bondage of fear. You can now let your smile change the world instead of the world changing your smile. You will refuse to lower your standards just to accommodate those who refuse to raise theirs.

Took Me a While

My Give-a-Damner was in full operation for much of my 20s and 30s.

Frankly, it didn't start to lose its power until well into my 40s. Believe me, once I knew it was there, which takes some time to discover, I tried everything to get rid of it. I tried pulling out the plug. I tried removing the batteries. I even tried stepping on it. But it still kept on working.

That thing took a licking and kept on ticking. Someone with a fully operational Give-a-Damner cares far too much about what others think of them. They live in a way that pleases others — at their own expense. They dress in a way that pleases others. They act in a way that pleases others. They say only what pleases others. They even die in a way that pleases others.

I was determined to destroy my Give-a-Damner by the next phase of my journey. Once I turned 40, I knew that it had to go. Because of my refusal to destroy it sooner, it took me experiencing some less than private humiliation in order to destroy that thing.

I am known to be a fashionista. I take that honor very seriously. People know that I love fashion and love to dress up. I'm the girl who wears pearls with a T-shirt and jeans. Well, one day, in a crowded church, I went to stand up after service ended. My skirt, which was too big for me, due to a recent weight loss, fell right to the ground. My bottom half (aka bum) was completely out. I was exposed. Everyone laughed at me as I bent down to pull it back up (along with my face).

My Give-a-Damner alarm went off big time. But I missed the point. The only reason why my skirt fell off was because it was too large for me. I had just lost 42 pounds, and I was in need of a shopping spree — that was all. I shouldn't have cared that others laughed at me. After all, it was pretty funny. Thank God, I had my good Sunday panties on that day!

It Influenced My Career Choice
If my Give-a-Damner wasn't working so well, I would have probably gone to school for Fashion Design instead of something more conservative like getting my Bachelors of Science in Management Information Systems. Does that even sound like me? No... but my Give-a-Damner told me to do that because others would see it as more reputable and responsible.

From the age of seven years old, I would sketch and draw clothes. At nine, I designed and made my own platform shoes. Fashion was my passion, but I let my Give-a-Damner talk me out of following that passion to FIT (Fashion Institute of Technology) or some other fashion school.

I thought that others would think less of me if I took a more artistic track. So I followed a path that I thought was the way I was expected to go. Meanwhile, most people would think that I was a real risk-taker. It was nothing compared to what I would have done had my Give-a-Damner not been working on full blast. I envied the people who lived free. Free of what others thought of them. They lived fully authentically, and that's what I wanted to do too — if it wasn't for that stupid Give-a-Damner.

But no matter how hard you try to get away with being perfect, or at least perceived that way, life has a way of keeping you humble and honest with yourself.

Life Ruled by the Give-a-Damner

I ended up, much to my Give-a-Damner's chagrin, experiencing all kinds of loss and failure all in front of everyone. The funniest part about the whole thing is that the people who I was trying to impress were having their own experiences and had no time or concern for mine. They weren't even paying attention! All this time I was trying to please people who don't even matter in the scheme of things. I had the nerve actually to care what perfect strangers who knew nothing about me had to say about me.

When people used to bring me gossip saying they heard this or that about me, I needed to feed my Give-a-Damner. I wanted to know who said what, when they said it, how they said it, and under what context it was said — as if it mattered. What good was that doing for me?

It brought me no benefit to know that perfect strangers said something silly about me. My Give-a-Damner was sucking the power out of me and causing my light to dim. As Marianne Williamson talks about in her poem, *"Our Greatest Fear,"* we do not serve the world by shrinking ourselves to make others feel comfortable. It is actually by us shining our light that we give others permission to do the same.

It took me most of the journey thus far to figure that one out.

I was so concerned with what you thought, that I could not serve you properly. I didn't say what I was sent to say or do because I cared what the world thought about it. What I was sent to do was to serve the world, and you can not serve the world and asks its permission at the same time. If it knew better, it wouldn't need you.

But I'm not that person any longer. It turns out that once I started doing me without regard for giving a damn, others started to follow suit. Being named a National Woman of Influence only came from me freeing myself from the self-imposed prison previously guarded by my Give-a-Damner.

> "A successful man is one who can lay a firm foundation
> with the bricks others have thrown at him."
> ~ David Brinkley

I know for sure that I let far too many people rent space in my head. I could have made a lot of money if I charged them for the time they spent there. What actually should have been done is serving them an eviction notice long ago. I should have repossessed my head. It was over-crowded. Too many people lived there. People who didn't deserve the space they were taking up. But that was on me and only on me.

No one can be there without your permission. I let them stay.

Living My Life, Not Someone Else's
Now that my Give-a-Damner is broken, when people try to bring me gossip that someone else has said about me, which is not very often any more (that's says something in and of itself), I shrug it off and don't even listen. It doesn't matter. That goes for the good and the bad. You can't differentiate because if you only wanted to hear the good that people had to say, your Give-a-Damner would still be in operation. Besides, it's virtually impossible to please all of the people all of the time.

Hey, a lion doesn't concern itself with the opinion of the sheep. He can't, after all. He must go about the business of being the king of the jungle. I was born to live my life, not someone else's. I was sent here to do a job. I was sent here to liberate the captives from the bondage of their minds. Do you think Jesus concerned himself with what others thought about him? No, because He was on a mission and so am I. And so should you be too.

Don't Think You Are,
Know You Are

"Stop acting so small.
You are the universe in ecstatic motion."
~ Rumi

The concept of "Don't think you are, know you are" was inspired again by the movie The Matrix. It was a concept Morpheus shared with Neo when he was training him to battle. Morpheus understood the importance of Neo not just thinking he was "the One" but actually knowing he was the One meant to save humankind. That's why when Neo went to visit the Oracle, she posed a very important question when the discussion turned to whether or not he was the One. She asked him what he thought about this.

Because he was unable to answer the question in the affirmative, from a place of knowing, she told him he was not the One. It was only later on in the film when Neo actually had a deep down "knowing" that he was the One that he became the One.

About Knowing

When we know something to be true about ourselves, we don't have to think it's true because there is a knowing. From that knowing, we act with an instinct and confidence that cannot be matched. Be established in knowing who you are. No matter what, deep down, you do know who and what you are. You've just had life happen and forgotten. This is often the reason we're frustrated because we are not living from our knowing.

Nothing around you can cause you to think anything other than what you know. A bird sitting on a tree is never afraid of a branch breaking because her trust in not in the branch, but in her own wings. The point of life is not to get somewhere; it is to notice that you are and have always been, already there. You know it but just forgot.

When you forget who you were and remember who you are, you will do the supernatural. It's not who you are that holds you back. It's who you think you're not. Who do you think you are? You must have a clear and concise answer to that question. Because, when the purpose of a thing is not clearly defined, abuse is inevitable.

You can only be to others what you are first to yourself.
- Neville Goddard

How Is Your Self-Image?
We cannot give expression to all the power within us until we awaken our spiritual natures, and realize exactly who we are and awake/recognize the God within us. Many people are suffering from an identity crisis. They just don't know who they are.

As your net worth is so closely tied to your self-worth, this is an important principle. If you have a poor self-image, you will settle for a poor life with poor relationships. You must believe that you are worthy of good things and good people in your life, in order to attract them in. With a strong, healthy self-image, you will be careful with who and what you allow into your life.

The people who are in your life right now are the ones you feel you deserve; this means that if you are in a dysfunctional marriage or relationship, somewhere deep down you feel you deserve this. In that case, we have some work to do on the inside of you. Perhaps some forgiveness (of yourself) is necessary so you can release yourself of past hurts and guilt. This will allow you to realize that you deserve better than what you are getting and giving to yourself right now.

This is not about other people; this is all about you. Your self-image will allow you to achieve your destiny. A poor self-image can derail you from a destiny of greatness. The fulfillment of your destiny is directly tied to who you believe yourself to be.

*"Can you remember who you were
before the world told you who you should be?"*
~ Danielle LaPorte

You are only as strong as your self-esteem. It is for that reason that I am so protective of the self-esteem of my children. I will not allow anyone — teachers, friends, and/or family — to adversely affect the self-esteem of my children. I am aware of how important a healthy self-image is to them living a maximized life of greatness and purpose.

Choose Your New State?
Here's the good news… if you don't like the events that are showing up in your life, you get to change them by controlling your thinking. If you don't like the state you are currently living in, pack up and move to a better, more desirable state. In this context, the state I am speaking of is your mental state.

There are many mental states in the universe of your mind. As Dr. Joe Vitale, says, the Universe is a catalog. Choose the experience you would like to have and express in your life, and by your thoughts, you can move to the state where that would inevitably show up. If you have been living in the state of despair, guess what! By changing your thoughts, you get to move to the state called joy.

Life is much more fun in that state. And once there, lock all the doors and refuse to move from that state.

"Feelings are much like waves, we can't stop them from coming but we can choose which one to surf."
- Jonatan Martensson

Don't Trust Your Feelings
While most people live by their feelings, it is not a smart way to go. The feelings are the effect and not the cause of why we "feel" a certain way about a relationship or a person or a situation. I never ask a client "how do you feel about this or that. Instead, I ask what are you thoughts about this or that.

51

For example, when we find that we "feel" differently about a person then we may have felt about them before. The fact is we first changed our thoughts about the person and then that person matched our thoughts. But the thoughts came first. What we are experiencing (feeling) is the results of our thoughts.

The Gift of Right Thinking
Life continues to give us gifts. The gifts are opportunities to rise higher in our consciousness. Unless we open up the gifts and follow the instructions contained within, we will get more gifts, but they will grow in intensity. If you persist in right thinking — even when your outer senses are not showing it yet — you will absolutely get there. This is because as you think in your heart, you must become.

Break the Shell

"Emancipate yourselves from mental slavery.
None but ourselves can free our minds."
~ Marcus Garvey

How does a caterpillar become a butterfly? It spins its own cocoon and then breaks out of its protective shell. Disturbing or tampering with the caterpillar inside of its cocoon risks botching the transformation process. This is the key to the butterfly's future. It must break out on its own.

Essentially, in the legal sense, the caterpillar must be pro se. Pro se is a Latin term used in the legal field which means for one's self. The caterpillar must do this alone. It must want to fly so much that it's willing to give up being a caterpillar.

You are the exact same way. To become a successful adult, who is living a productive life of purpose, you must go through a metamorphosis. You must escape mediocrity. You must desire excellence so much that you're willing to give up the comfort that mediocrity offers.

The Metamorphosis Process

Many years ago, I was going through a difficult time in my business. I couldn't get help from the people I thought were supposed to help me. I was struggling to put my projects altogether, to make them successful. I was frustrated and felt alone. I was praying and yet did not "see" results.

A friend introduced me to a man named Bobby who touted himself as a prophet. Bobby traveled around the world delivering life-changing prophesies to people who were desperate for answers. My friend called Bobby up and put him on the phone with me.

Within seconds of hearing my voice, this prophet told me some chilling facts about my life that no one else would have possibly known. He was the real deal. He told me I was in a cocoon and needed to go through my own metamorphosis process, and I would need to do it alone. He told me it would be painful, but it was a necessary process for my successful transformation. I had to break my way out, he said. He assured me that if I submitted to the process, I was going to do great things in the world, and I would soar to heights that few would ever see. Bobby's prophecy to me was spot on. My pain had a purpose.

Everything he said has either happened or is happening right now, and I now share that same advice with you. You may be feeling like you're in a tight spot. You may be frustrated by the lack of help you're getting from people who you feel may be in a position to help you but are not. It's OK. You're simply going through your transformation.

It's impossible to be what you're supposed to be without going through this metamorphosis. It's hard for those who love you to watch you go through the process because the tendency is to want to help you out — but they cannot. It will hinder your progress.

The Little Boy & The Butterfly
There's a story of the little boy who discovered a cocoon in his backyard. He noticed that the butterfly was struggling to break out of its shell. The boy ran inside the house, grabbed some scissors, and decided he was going to assist the butterfly. The boy gently held the delicate cocoon in his hand, and he carefully cut the cocoon along an already exposed crack — which the butterfly had made itself. He made a large enough incision for the butterfly to get out of the shell. The butterfly was then free, but there was a problem — its wings did not work. It was incapable of flight.

The little boy had been eager and excited to help the struggling butterfly. However, unbeknownst to him, the butterfly needed to break out on its own in order for its wings to work effectively. This was a necessary part of its growth process.

"God grant me the serenity to accept the people I cannot change, the courage to change the one I can, and the wisdom to know it's me."
- Unknown Author

54

Shutting the Door
There's another interesting similarity that we have to the caterpillar. When it's time for the caterpillar to mature, it retreats to and wanders away from its normal routine. It finds a sheltered, safe spot in which to pupate, or transform into an adult. You may find the need to do the same.

For me, when I'm going through a transformation, it is often important to "shut the door" on people, places, and things and to find a safe (and secret) place to transform. Remember, Clark Kent always had to go behind a rock or a wall or inside of a phone booth in order to transform into Superman. He didn't just do it out in the open in front of everyone. He had to "shut the door."

When you're working on something major, keep your plans to yourself until you have solidified them in your own mind. Treat them as an embryo that's formed in the dark, out of sight. Why do you think babies are formed in the darkness of the womb and not outside of the body where everyone can see? Because if you saw that seed forming and developing, perhaps you would lack respect for it and would have trouble believing that it would eventually turn out to be a beautiful baby.

Have you ever seen those sonogram pictures when the fetus in only about eight weeks old? To tell the truth, they do look like aliens from another planet. But somehow in God's infinite mastery, over time, that strange looking thing becomes an adorable newborn baby. We've got to trust the process, but that often means shutting the door on outsiders.

Throughout the Bible, the world's greatest self-help book, you'll find stories about times when miracles were about to be performed. It was usually done only after the people involved "shut the door" on outsiders who were not committed to the process or who wouldn't understand what or why things were happening.

When you're looking to accomplish something that may appear crazy or perhaps impossible to other people, you must go inside and shut the door behind you. You have to protect that thing from the intense scrutiny of those who may not agree with or believe in what you're doing. I firmly believe in the concept that some things are on a "need to know basis only." Especially when a project or vision is at its infancy stages, it's important to protect it as you would your newborn baby. You don't let everyone and anyone hold your baby, especially those without clean hands.

Protect your projects and dreams in the same way. Eventually, you will fly — I promise.

Just Do You Very Well

"The privilege of a lifetime is being who you are."
~ Joseph Campbell

Why try to fit in when you were born to stand out? The privilege of a lifetime is to be who you really are. The one without the masks and pretense. The one who is perfect just the way you are. You, my friend, are a designer original who has been marvelously and masterfully made. Don't try to be anything else, just do you. And do that very well. That is what makes you unique.

Whatever you're working with — short or tall, curvy or slim, curly or straight — you must work that thing. Love the skin you're in.

"How many cares one loses when one decides
not to be something but to be someone."
~ Gabrielle "Coco" Chanel

As soon as possible, discover what you were sent here to do, do that right away, and do it very well. Don't worry about the money. Where God guides, he provides. You wouldn't have been given the vision without the provision. Just do you. If you're truly called, then you're also truly equipped to do what you need to do. It's built into the system that way.

Everything you need is already in the package. You don't need to look for anything outside of yourself. All you need is already inside. Batteries are included.

Vocation vs. Occupation

One major source of frustration for believers is trying to answer the question, "What am I here for?" or "What am I supposed to do with my life?" That's a loaded question without an easy answer. What I can tell you, however, is to focus more on your vocation and less on your occupation. The word "vocation" actually comes from the Latin word vocare, which means "calling."

In contemporary culture, I like to say that our occupation is our hustle, while our vocation is our flow. When you're called to do something, it comes easily to you. You don't have to struggle to do it; it just flows. Only you know what that thing is.

I usually tell my coaching clients that their vocation is the thing that they would do for free, and often do. It's that thing that comes so naturally to you, it's like breathing. That is your vocare, also referred to as your "gift." It's that special thing that was given to you and only you. It's often overlooked by you because it literally is so easy and natural that you don't even recognize that everyone else is not gifted with that. Only you are.

If you have a strong desire to do something, know that the desire is your revelation of the purpose for why you were born. A desire, from the Latin word desiderare, means to long for, wish for, demand or expect. But its root meaning means "from the stars." That desire in your heart came from the stars. It's a gift to you and only you. Open it up and use it — for your own benefit and for the rest of us.

If you're different than everyone else around you, congratulations! That's great news because your future is in your difference. Your difference creates your assignment. When you're where you are assigned, you have no rivals.

My Vocare Kept Finding Me

I thought that I had cheated on my gift(s) for the longest time. I avoided — or at least tried to avoid — doing what I was destined, purposed, to do because I didn't realize that my gifts will make room for me. I thought that I had to do something else to make money (my hustle) while I was working my gifts (my flow) on the side. I put my gift on the back burner,

thinking that when I made enough money I would eventually be able to do what I was destined to do full-time. Bad idea.

Instead, I couldn't hide from my gifts — no matter how I tried. No matter what industry (occupation) I was employed in, I ended up coaching, counseling, enlightening, enriching and entertaining people. That is what I was born to do. It doesn't matter what occupation I was assigned to; I was there to share my gifts, my vocare.

I have somehow found a way to do what I was purposed to do in every job, business, industry or career I was involved in. I later learned that I was not employed, I was deployed. I was placed on assignment.

I have been involved in some active capacity in the following industries, but not limited to (mostly as the business owner/partner):

Artist Management and Development
Automotive Sales and Distribution
Coaching
College Recruiting Service
Compensation Plan Design and Development
Customer Service Training
Diversity Training and Consultation
Employee Relations
Entertainment
Event Planning
Fashion Design and Merchandising
Human Resources
Hypno-Therapy
Infrastructure Design
Interior Design
Jewelry
Legal
Limousine Service
Management
Marketing
Modeling
Mortgages

Music
Non-profits (Arts, Education)
Radio
Radio Frequency Engineering
Real Estate Development and Construction
Restauranteur
Sales
Sports Management
Telecommunications
Television Production
Title Company
Training and Development

In each of those careers or occupations, I couldn't help but bring forth what was inside of me — what was purposed for me to do. There were always people to inspire and encourage, and I would find them — or they found me.

I was placed on assignment in multiple occupations, but my specific purpose and charge never changed. The fact is our first and foremost instruction from the Creator is to be fruitful. To be fruitful means we are to produce, be productive. I realize now that none of those experiences that I had and are still having, were/are a waste of my time. I was being productive. I was fulfilling my assignment.

Some people are placed on assignment by doing one sole thing as their entire career, profession or life's work. That is not my reality.

Don't Waste Your Time
Never, ever get complacent once you have found your vocare (or calling). Use every day you have to go farther than you have been. You are called to be more. Be more today than you were yesterday. At the end of each day, ask yourself, "Was I productive?" It doesn't matter whether you made mistakes, as long as you learned from them. If you did, you were fruitful. You are becoming more, and that is the point.

Your calling and gifts are intended by God for you to share with others in this world, in this dispensation in time in which you were

60

placed. Look at the great artists, singers, musicians of our time. These creative people may not be curing cancer but at the same time they have arguably saved a lot of lives through their gifts. There are so many talented lyricists that surely saved mine with their words.

I'm surely glad they were not trying to be anything else other than what they were designed to be. They are fruitful in their own way. Every individual has a Divine purpose. There are things only you can offer to this world and we're all waiting on you to do it. Don't waste your time being anything other than what you were born to be. Just do you very well.

Our Default Settings

Today so many of our electronics come with default settings. Those are the settings that the factory determined were perhaps the most commonly used or preferred settings for most people. Usually, the factory settings were set up to get the maximum use out of the product and were exactly how it was designed to work best. Then the end-user gets a hold of the product and begins to customize it to exactly how he/she would like it to work.

Often, our customization is not in the best interest of the product's longevity or optimal performance. This is the way our lives are.

We were each born with a specific purpose to accomplish a particular mission. We come into this dispensation in time knowing exactly who and what we are, with our entire factory settings firmly programmed. But as we begin to grow up and are exposed to the environment, we begin to alter the intentions of the Creator. We begin to learn the ways of the world and forget who we really are.

It's my belief that we are all on a journey of returning back to our factory default settings. A place where we know exactly who and what we are. Our identity is secure, and we are back to our supernatural powers. Maybe it's time for a factory reset. A factory reset is when you forget who you were and remember who you really are and were intended to be. Press reset and be fruitful.

"If you are afraid of failure you don't deserve to be successful."
-Charles Barkley

Do We Fear Our Power?

Have the courage to be you. The courage to be you is the greatest quality one can ever possess. We seem to spend far too much time and money trying to be someone else. Perhaps it's trying to be like our sibling, our parent, our friend or even a celebrity. Perhaps it's Michael Jordan or Beyoncé that you admire. Some say that if it is a positive role model, then it's OK for you to want to be like them. Well, I beg to differ.

Don't get me wrong; role models are great. It just depends on how you use that model. Let's say you always admired your older sister, big brother or best friend, and you wanted to be just like them. Perhaps you cut your hair, colored it, borrowed or bought clothes just like theirs, but still you did not become them.

Let me save you a lot of time and money. No matter how hard you try, you cannot become someone else. So don't waste another moment trying. Every time you copy someone, you're cheapening yourself and discounting your own unique value. Let people inspire you but don't copy them. Focus on being the best you that you can be. Just do you.

Why is it that we fear being our true selves around others? Is Marianne Williamson right in suggesting that it is not our inadequacies that we fear, but instead we actually fear our immense power and ability? The reality is that no one ever points out our power to us; they seem only to point out our inadequacies. Imagine a world where we all embraced our unique powers and talents without fear.

What are we afraid of anyhow? It seems easier to me to design and develop yourself into the best you that you can be. It's perfectly acceptable to be inspired by others you admire and select attributes that you like in them. Allow that to inspire you, as you do the work of your own personal development. Because you, my friend, are a designer original, and you should have the courage to be yourself.

My Fixation on Farrah

When I was young, my first celebrity idol was Farrah Fawcett. I wanted to be Farrah Fawcett, not like her, to actually be her. Well, in retrospect, I probably wanted to be Jill Monroe, the character Farrah played in Charlie's Angels in the late 70s. At that time, we didn't have tabloids, reality shows or social media to tell us all of the gory details of celebrity's personal lives. So all we knew about was the fabulous, glamorous life she lived back then. Farrah was married to The Six Million Dollar Man Steve Austin (at that time that was a lot of money), portrayed by hunky Lee Majors. Farrah was strong yet sexy, powerful yet feminine and delicate. She had a mega-watt smile, and everyone loved her.

Now let's examine the challenges of me wanting to be Farrah Fawcett. Farrah was a blonde, white female with sparkling blue eyes. She wore a size 2, had small, perky boobs, and adoring fans from far and wide. Which of the attributes that Farrah possessed could I possibly have had the chance of becoming?

I would say that besides being female, at that time the similarities pretty much stopped there. Even at 12 years old, I was far better endowed than Farrah, so the small perky boobs were already out of the question. I also had no chance of becoming a white female with blonde hair and blue eyes, although I did try the blonde hair a few times after that. However, what I could do (and did) was take what I admired about Farrah and her character Jill Monroe and I incorporated that into the development of me, Shelley Roxanne.

I soon realized that when we are ourselves, not trying to be anyone else, we bring something unique and wonderful into the world that never existed here before and never will again. If you had a chance to see photos from my past, you will find the Farrah influence — mostly in the late 70s and early 80s when I wore the Farrah Fawcett flip in my naturally curly, medium length brown hair. I had a perky personality and used what I was given to work with for the rest.

Bottom line: I was the best Shelley I could be and didn't try to become Farrah Fawcett in the long run. Besides, Farrah had the Farrah Fawcett thing down pretty well.

Once I had the courage to be myself, I eventually became someone who others emulated. Now I see people all the time who are inspired by me. It humbles me immensely. When I see that, it inspires me right back and allows me to become more of myself, a better, finer version of me. Having been named a National Women of Influence was such a big honor for me because I appreciated all the wonderful people who had influenced me throughout my life, and still do. Therefore, I take the honor with great humility and great responsibility.

No One Can Do It Better

Now, thanks to the celebrity tabloids and reality shows, we know much too much about the actual lives of today's celebrities. As a part of being in the music industry, I've had the honor of meeting many of the nation's top celebrities. So let me assure you, you really wouldn't want to be them. I hear you, you're probably thinking that you could deal with the huge mansions, fancy cars, pricy clothes, exotic vacations, adoring fans, etc.

All that may seem great, but you have no idea of the price they pay daily to have all of those things. Remember, to whom much is given, much is expected. Be sure you can meet those expectations, especially your own. My suggestion is, have the courage to be you. Besides, no one else can do it better, not even Farrah.

Don't Talk to Yourself like That

"For life makes no mistakes and always gives man that which man first gives himself."
~ Neville Goddard

If you're going to change your life and eliminate frustration, you must first change your conversation. To live an optimistic lifestyle, you must watch what you say to and about - YOU. The words we use are critical to our success or failure. Words have creative power, so make sure you create what you can live with. Positive thinking alone will not change your circumstances. Positive thinking may change you, but your tongue changes your circumstances.

You see, the words you use, both out loud and when you talk to yourself, actually help to create your experience. If you think talking to yourself makes you crazy, I would say that if you don't talk to you then who will? Your speech is indicative of your self-esteem. I can talk to a perfect stranger for 5 minutes and tell you whether their self-esteem is healthy or not, just by the quality of their conversation.

Your internal communication is critical. The quality of the words you speak to yourself will determine the quality of your life. Frankly, you are the first to hear the words that come from your mouth.

Which Dog Do You Feed?

According to behavioral psychologists, as much as 77% of our self-talk is negative. And I suspect that figure is for the average person, so imagine the really negative people. No wonder so many people are suffering from depression and are on mood-altering medication. The negative self-talk comes from bad programming of the computer (your subconscious mind).

There is an old Native American story of two Natives sitting by a campfire. One was a wise elder of the tribe, the other a young warrior. The wise elder Native tells the young warrior, "There are two dogs that live inside me. One is a gray dog that is negative and filled with fear and anger. The other is a white dog that is positive and filled with love. The gray dog is constantly trying to attack the white dog." The young warrior said to the elder, "Which dog wins?" The wise elder answers, "Whichever one I feed the most."

Which of your dogs are you feeding the most? I realize that it is often easier to feed the gray dog, which is negative and filled with fear and anger. That's because negativity is more readily available and can be picked up anywhere. Feeding the white dog, the positive one who is filled with love and optimism, is sometimes harder because his food is not as easily accessible in everyday society. You may have to search and dig for the positive, but I promise you it is out there.

You are actually reading it now, so eat up.

Words & Their Out-Picture

Researchers say the tongue is the most exercised and, therefore, the strongest muscle in the human body. Have you ever been told to bite your tongue? When you were younger and used inappropriate language, did an elder tell you that they were going to wash your mouth out with soap? Why would they think to do that? Perhaps they knew the importance of what you say and the corresponding out-picture you will see in your own life as a result.

I actually learned that words can create an atmosphere. You can create a loving atmosphere in your home by your tongue. Early in our marriage, Jeff and I went house shopping with a realtor to purchase our first home. We went to one particular house, and as soon as the realtor opened the door, as I stood right in the foyer I could sense that words were spoken there that caused strife in the home. I asked the realtor if a divorce had happened there. She told me that a divorce was precisely the reason the house was for sale. The residence had not even been lived in, but it had an atmosphere of arguments taking place there. She later clarified that the owners of the house split up during the building of the house, and the bickering resulted in divorce and; therefore, they had to sell the home.

The good news, and you know I always have to give you the good news, is that what was started with words can be turned around with words. We ended up buying that house and turned around the spirit of it with our words. We even asked the owner to pray with us, which he surprisingly gladly obliged, in order to speak blessing over the house and everyone that came in it.

Not one person walked through that house during the eight years we lived there who didn't express how warm, loving and comfortable they felt while in our home. The atmosphere shifted. There was something in the atmosphere now that made people want to stay there. Trust me that's true because we had family who came to stay for a weekend and didn't leave for four years! My point is that words changed the atmosphere.

Our words became life, and that house is still one the favorite places for each of my sons because such beautiful memories were made there.

"The difference between the right word and the almost right word
is like the difference between lightning and the lightning bug."
~ Mark Twain

Affirming What You Want

Be diligent in using the power of the tongue to create a positive force in your life. If you plan or desire to do great things, but you don't speak affirmatively as it relates to those plans, it will be virtually impossible to accomplish the goal. With your lack of words, you have put limitations on what is possible with your tongue. You will never rise above your own confession.

"Let no corrupt communication proceed out of your mouth,
but that which is good to the use of edifying,
that it may minister grace unto the hearers."
~ Ephesians 4:29

For example, if you say things like "I don't have a good memory," "I'm not good with numbers," "I am prone to sore throats in the winter," or "Things will never change"— all those things can and must come to pass in your life experience because you have commanded them to with your words.

The Bible tells us to "call those things that be not as though they were." (See Romans 4:17.) This means that if you don't want to be prone to colds in the winter, don't "say" it. If you don't want to forget things, declare in your words that you have a good memory. Etc., etc. Let the weak say "I am strong!". (see Joel 3:10)

> "He who guards his mouth and
> his tongue keeps himself from calamity."
> ~ Proverbs 21:23

Don't use I AM in Vain

This is another secret within a secret. If you can change this one thing, you will see an immediate shift in your life's experience. Here it is.

There is only one place in the Bible when God says His name. It's when he told Moses when asked "who should I say sent me, what is your name". God's answer to Moses was, "tell them I AM has sent me to you". So let's examine this further. Logically, God is telling Moses that his name is "I AM". Which means that every time we say I AM, we are talking about God. Well, it doesn't take a rocket scientist to figure out that if we walk around saying, I AM sick, we are saying God is sick. Or if we say, I AM broke, we are saying God is broke.

Sounds to me like a serious violation of the third commandment that prohibits us from taking the name of the Lord in vain.

The Tongue as a Creative Force

With words, we build our world. When Vanessa Williams, actress and former Miss America, was born, her parents put on her birth announcement these words: Here She Is… Miss America. This is a perfect example of calling something "that was not" as if it were. What Vanessa's parents called her at birth is exactly what we "called" her some 20 years

later when she accepted the crown of Miss America.

The Williams' used their tongue as a creative force and called something into existence and; therefore, it came to pass for their daughter. It was Vanessa's destiny because her parents commanded it to be so. Just like Mr. and Mrs. Williams, speak what you want into existence.

At first, it may feel like a lie but you must speak your wishes into your life. Trust me on this one; according to your faith (demonstrated by your words), it will Be unto You! You will have to convince the most important person of this truth, and that person is you. Just keep speaking the truth, not the facts. The facts don't count. If it's not in line with the word of God, it's not truth no matter what the evidence appears to say. The brain simply "believes" what you tell it most. And what you tell it about you, it will create.

Do you have an audio device, a smartphone or the like that you use when you walk, work out, clean or just relax? If so, I suggest you record affirmations in your own voice that are calling out all those things you want into your life in an affirmative way.

"For by thy words thou shalt be justified,
and by thy words thou shalt be condemned."
~ Matthew 12:37

Apply words that are encouraging and positive towards every situation — no matter how it looks — if you expect to see positive results. The fact is, your life experience is entirely up to you, and it's subject to your tongue. You can either have what you say or, like most people, simply say what you have. It's up to you.

This is so very important, especially the words we speak to our children. The words we speak to them help build their self-esteem or tear it down for life. Correction and direction without love neither corrects nor encourages. The Book of Job teaches us that the ear tests words as the tongue tastes food. What do your children taste — the bitter or the sweet?

I've witnessed a mother telling her son, "You're no good, just like your father." She went on to tell him he would never amount to anything, just like his father didn't amount to anything. Now do I believe that this mother intentionally wanted to harm her son? Absolutely not. But she is harming him, harming him very badly. That mother is speaking prophetically over her son. He will spend a lifetime living up, or down, to her words.

Only the Good Die Young

"Don't be too moral. You may cheat yourself out
of much life, so aim above morality.
Be not simply good, be good for something."
~ Henry David Thoreau

As a child of the 80s, I used to listen to a lot of Billy Joel, a very popular singer-songwriter at that time. He was, and is a great talent. I have always been a fan of great lyricists, and as far as I am concerned, Billy Joel is one of the best.

I grew up the daughter of a well-known family in a small town, in what anyone from south of The George Washington Bridge would call, Upstate New York. I could certainly identify with that Catholic girl that Billy Joel sang about in his mega-hit "Only the Good Die Young." I just couldn't wrap my head around why only the "good" would die young? Isn't that the complete opposite of what we're taught? I thought that the better you were, the longer you would live. But I did realize that trying to be what I call a "goodie goodie" was definitely a huge problem for me. Maybe I should call this Secret - Only the Goodie Goodie Die Young.

You know those "goodie goodie" types. The ones who try to be perfect, look perfect, act perfect, and say the perfect thing. Those people. The fun suckers. They suck the fun out of every situation in their demand for perfection from themselves and everyone else around them.

Are You Religious?
The concept of being religious is often misconstrued. To do something religiously means to do it regularly perhaps due to some sense of duty. To consider one religious often means assuming that this person is devout or pious, being totally committed to their belief. Stereotypically religious

people are believed to be holy, saintly and worst - judgmental. For some reason, I never wanted to be referred to as religious. It just carries with it such a stigma.

The religious people I knew never had any fun. They were bored and boring. The woman didn't wear makeup or pants and God forbid they'd want to catch a movie. It was forbidden. While, on the surface, they seemed content, on the inside they were miserable. The girls I grew up with who were considered by others to be religious were far more promiscuous than the girls who were not. These girls used to sneak boys into the house when their parents were away and did things the non-religious girls wouldn't even think of doing.

Religious vs. Spiritual

Religion lives by logic and reason, not by faith. Religion centers around do's and don'ts - mostly don'ts. Religious people are big on what others should and should not do. But they themselves do not demonstrate the righteousness to which they espouse.

Chapter Three of Second Timothy literally instructs that you should not have anything to do with people who hold to an outward form of godliness but deny its power. It says to stay clear of these people. Said another way, if they don't walk their talk, don't hang with them.

To be Spiritual, on the other hand simply means your mind, heart and actions are in alignment. Regardless of your own B.S.

Low-Risk Living

One of the greatest detriments to trying to be so goodie goodie is that you tend to take less risks. I probably took far too little risks in my earlier days because I was suffering from the dis-ease to please. I was far too concerned with being perfect and conforming to the expectations of others. My greatest fear at that time was that someone, anyone, wouldn't like me or that I would disappoint my parents by making a — dare I say it — mistake.

When Billy Joel so eloquently told that girl in his song that the stain glassed curtain she was hiding behind was limiting her life, boy could I relate. You certainly are missing all the fun that life has to offer if you're on some ridiculous, unattainable quest to be perfect. It took time for me to realize that well-behaved women rarely made history. You've got to be willing to break the rules, rock the boat, and color outside the lines.

For you "religious" types, know this: low-risk living is a sin. I know it's hard to hear, but you're continuing to sin if you're playing it safe. He who risks nothing does nothing, has nothing, is nothing, and becomes nothing. You may pray regularly, go to church or temple weekly, and are kind to others. However, if you're not taking risks on a regular basis, you are sinful. Low-risk living is not honoring God. Sitting on the sidelines of life is no way to live. Get in the game.

> *"Until you've lost your reputation, you never realize*
> *what a burden it was or what freedom really is."*
> ~ Margaret Mitchell

Your Life Should Match Your God

As a matter of fact, God calls it evil when you walk and live below your potential. Some of the most disappointing things I've seen over the years were when I encountered evangelists, ministers or clergy members who didn't take risks in their own lives and ministries.

Yet they'd stand from their pulpits and stages and tell us that "all things are possible to those who believe." Sounds good, but do they believe that themselves? You must practice what you preach. God is BIG. If you know this to be true, than you also know that your goals, dreams, and your life should match your God.

Simply, the nature of the word "desire" sums up this point. The word desire in Latin means from the Father. If you have been given desires that are noble and righteous, no matter how audacious, they come from the Father. It's your responsibility and yours alone to take things higher and to another level. You were given the assignment to do what you desire in your heart to do. It was placed there for a reason. The desire is the nudge that tells you what you need to do. If your spouse, your parents, your partner or your friends don't see it, that's because they're not supposed to or it would have been a desire given to them. Instead it was given to you. If we don't do the work we were meant to do, it will forever remain undone because the assignment was exclusively ours.

*"Forget safety. Live where you fear to live.
Destroy your reputation. Be notorious."*
~ Rumi

No Regrets
Persist… because with an idea, determination and the right tools, you can do great things. Let your instincts, your intellect, and your heart guide you. Try things, do things today that your future self will thank you for. While I'm not a fan of regrets — because I believe we learn from everything that happens to us — I probably, in retrospect, should have laughed more with the sinners and cried less with the saints as Billy Joel suggested to Virginia.

PART. THREE

PRIVATE
PRACTICES

Fear Not

*"Fear is the cheapest room in the house.
I would like to see you living in better conditions."*
~ Hafiz

FEAR is a big one — the worst of the four letter words. In my opinion, it's what causes the most frustration for the believer. Fear is the oldest and strongest emotion of humankind. Living in fear is a choice and not a very good one I might add. Fear is a distortion of what was once fearlessness.

When it comes to Fear, I know how you feel, I felt the same way. And this is what I found. Fear will take you further than you wanna go, keep you longer than you wanna stay, and charge you more than you wanna pay!

Dealing with the Illusion of Fear

Fear is often defined as an acronym with its meaning being False Evidence Appearing Real (F.E.A.R). If it appears real, it can have the very same impact as if it were real. Think of it this way. If you were on a virtual roller coaster, you would experience the same emotion as if you were on a real one. Your roller coaster train may not be moving at all, but it feels real. That virtual roller coaster is an example of False Evidence Appearing Real. Remember, we've already determined that it's not what it looks like.

How often do we experience an illusion related to an obstacle that feels in every aspect to be very real, but is not in fact real? What gives it that real feeling is us. We give it life and energy and assist it in feeling real to us. I've found that the only way to overcome fear is not to resist it, but to replace it.

Replace your fear with faith. If you resist fear, it will persist and grow bigger. Don't do that. Simply replace fear with uncompromising faith. Faith in the truth, faith in God, faith in yourself. But to do this, you must know who you truly are. We often tolerate fear because somewhere deep down we think that we deserve what is happening to us. This is part of the identity crisis that most Frustrated Believers suffer from. But it's all B.S. (Belief Systems).

"Fear grows in darkness.
If you think there's a bogeyman around, turn on the light."
~ Dorothy Thompson

You've Got to Be Carefully Taught

We know that God has not given us the spirit of fear, so where does it come from? I suggest that it's programming. You've probably noticed that the things you're afraid of or fear are the same things your parents and their parents and people from your past also feared. Fear, therefore, is hereditary, and it is taught or learned. Well, everything that is learned can be un-learned.

There's a famous show tune from the 1949 Rodgers and Hammerstein musical South Pacific that says it all. The main idea is captured in the title, "You've Got to Be Carefully Taught." The song reminds us how hate and fear can be "drummed into" our little ears and taught to us as young children.

As I wrote in the last chapter, during my childhood, I surely was taught to fear what others thought of me. I grew up in a well-known family in my small town. My father and mother had spent their lives serving the community and developing a reputation that was above reproach.

As the Mayor of the village, my father was well regarded by everyone — not just in the town but throughout the state. Even those who were on the other side of the aisle politically still highly respected him as someone with class and integrity. My mother was the ultimate First Lady. She stood by her man and was in her own right well loved by all. Our family name was highly respected.

On the one hand, that was a good thing. In retrospect, I realize that it caused me to take fewer risks myself. I felt I had to maintain a reputation that was painstakingly built by my parents. Everything that I did, I was concerned about how that would reflect upon Mom and Dad. My deepest fear was to disappoint or embarrass them. As a result, I stayed "in my lane" and didn't explore things or take major risks. I didn't want my behavior to reflect adversely upon our good family name. I was fearful.

I was more concerned with being liked than with being myself and fulfilling my assignment. I felt that the name belonged to them and that it was not my right to risk tarnishing it. Not that this would have happened, but the risk was far too great for me to take at that time. The harsh reality is that if you're afraid of and/or concerned about what others think of you, you will invariably not do or try things. But these very things may be necessary for your progress or to fulfill your destiny. You can miss an opportunity out of the fear of failure or of not pleasing someone else — or maybe everyone else.

"It takes courage to grow up and become who you really are."
~ E.E. Cummings

Finding Our Courage
What is courage anyway? Courage is not the absence of fear, but rather the judgment that something else is more important than fear. The trouble is that we often die many times before death overtakes us. So many people are running from something that's not even chasing them. What you need to do is find something that you want more than you're afraid of that other thing.

I doubt that you're afraid of failing because failure is something most people know how to do. It's success that is a foreign concept to most of us. But failure is the womb for success. It is the birthplace of success. It's where it all begins.

"Death is not the biggest fear we have; our biggest fear
is taking the risk to be alive – the risk to be alive and express what we really are."
~ Don Miguel Ruiz

I can speak passionately about fear because this is the one area that I had to confront before releasing this book. Even in my adult life, I suffered from the fear of not pleasing others, aka the dis-ease to please. Well, I had it and had it bad. I was so concerned with pleasing others that I missed the mark so many times when it came to fulfilling my life's purpose. You can't possibly be your best self and please God, who created you when you're focusing more on pleasing others.

I am here to tell you that I was so afraid of what people would think of me that I wasn't living fully. It wasn't until I confronted fear in its ugly face that I realized this did not serve me. Because of it, I said things I shouldn't have said and didn't say things I should have said. Because of it, I spent time with people I didn't like and missed out on time with the people I really liked. I went where I should not have gone and didn't go where I should have, all because of fear. Well, those days are over for me.

In the past, I knew in my heart what I should have done but I was paralyzed by fear. Fear that you would not see me, Shelley Roxanne, as perfect and flawless, without a spot or wrinkle. How ridiculous is that? I was so concerned with what you thought of me that I didn't even like what I was becoming— weak, fearful and insignificant, not to mention disobedient. Disobedient because I was "called" to be fearless, to be great, to inspire others, and I couldn't accomplish my calling while remaining in fear. It is impossible to change something, anything when you are afraid of it.

"Don't give in to your fears. If you do, you won't be able to talk to your heart."
— Paulo Coelho, *The Alchemist*

Not long ago, I had a bout with Fear. A dear friend was dealing with a personal situation and was fearful about its outcome. I was groping for answers of what to tell my friend because their situation did "look" pretty grim. Anyway, I was at one of Taylor's swim meets. There were at least 1000+ people there.

Out of the blue, a woman who I have never seen before - or again - walked up to me and asked if she could speak with me. She told me she was lead to pray for someone, but she didn't know who the person was.

She asked me, a perfect stranger if I would stand and pray with her for this person. As she began to pray, she spoke of exactly the situation that my friend was dealing with. She said that everything was going to turn out fine for this person and that this was a necessary part of their journey. She again told me she had no idea who she was praying for, but I knew exactly who it was.

God in his loving kindness, sent an angel to me to pray and remind me that He is with me always and that I am never alone and have absolutely nothing to Fear.

Fear vs. Wisdom
A little clarification is needed at this point. It's a common misconception that a little fear is healthy or keeps you from danger. I argue that this is a big mistake. You must seek to eliminate ALL fear from your life. Others argue that such things as fearing to put our hand in fire or fearing speeding on an icy road are good fears. That is not fear; that is wisdom. It's not fear that prevents you from putting your hand in fire or from driving recklessly on an icy road; this is simply operating in wisdom.

It's important that you understand the difference between these two things. Wisdom means having the knowledge and understanding to recognize the right course of action and having the will and courage to follow it. Wisdom is a critical attribute for an optimist. Wisdom should be your goal, and you should do everything you can and pay whatever you must to get it. But don't confuse it with fear.

"How blessed is the man who finds wisdom, and the man who gains understanding.
For its profits are better than the profit of silver,
and its gain better than fine gold. She is more precious than jewels;
and nothing you desire compares with her. Long life is in her right hand; in her
left hand are riches and honor. Her ways are pleasant ways, and all her paths are
peace. She is a tree of life to those who take hold of her, and happy are all who
hold her fast."
~ Proverbs 3:13-18

Knowing God Is with Us

Let us cross over to the other side away from fear. Consider this parable. One day, Jesus told his disciples, "Let us cross over to the other side" (written about in both the Book of Luke and the Book of Mark). Every time Jesus says that you can rest assured that something is about to "jump off." Let us cross over to the other side was a signal that it was time for a promotion (or change), an opportunity to advance. It was time to grow and develop to the next level. It was time for the disciples to exercise their faith — to work it out.

On this particular day, they all got into a boat and set out to cross over the water. However, shortly after they got comfortable in the boat, Jesus went to sleep. It is my belief that he went to sleep on purpose. He knew what was about to happen, and he was resting in the knowledge that all would be well.

Soon after they were sailing, the winds and the water became fierce and strong, and the men were seemingly in great danger. I say "seemingly" because as long as Jesus was with them, they could not possibly be in any real danger — whether he was asleep or not. However, water was beating against the boat, and it started to fill up the ship. Plus, the winds were contrary. Soon the boat was nearly swamped. The disciples were fearful. They woke up Jesus and basically accused him of not caring about them.

At this point, it became obvious that fear took over because they began to panic. I can only imagine how they felt at that moment. The situation seemed dire. I'm sure you can relate to times in your life when things looked really bad, and you wondered how you were going to get out of a situation. You probably thought God had forgotten about you or was asleep during your crisis. You, like the disciples, probably panicked in the midst of the storm that seemingly would destroy you.

What the disciples failed to recognize was that when He said, "Let us cross over," that meant that they were not alone. God, through the form of Jesus, was with the disciples the entire time, even though he appeared to be asleep. So if "your crossing over experience" is starting a new business, traveling the world, running for office, starting a family, joining a team, facing a trial, or even dealing with an illness or a challenging financial crisis... know that God is with you, even if you think He is asleep. No evil can come to you. You need never be afraid.

A Demonstration of Courage

I'm most fond of the demonstration of courage displayed by the three Hebrew boys — Hananiah, Mishael and Azariah — written about in the book of Daniel. In this book, these three boys were warned by the King against not complying with a law he had instituted. If they did not comply, he said they would be thrown into a burning fiery furnace heated up seven times hotter than normal. But the problem was that the law the King had instituted was in direct contradiction with the boys' beliefs.

You could say they were caught between a rock and a hard place. Certainly the threat of being thrown into a fiery furnace if you refused to go against your own beliefs would not even be a question for you and me today. The fear of death would probably win out in most circumstances.

Without fear, the three boys refused to be compromised in the face of the threat of certain death. They did not fear. And as a result, although the circumstances did call for them actually to be thrown into the furnace, they were not harmed one bit. Rather, they were not affected at all. They were bound up with ropes and thrown into the furnace, but not even a hair on their heads was singed nor were their clothes discolored. They didn't even smell of smoke. As a matter of fact, the only thing that burned off was the rope that had tied them up. Right in the midst of the fire, they were made free. All because fear did not bound them.

After the King witnessed this great demonstration of faith, he had them come out of the furnace. Impressed with their demonstration of confidence and conviction, the King changed his mind towards the boys. As a result of them standing on their conviction, the King decided he would promote the three boys. Notably, the people who conspired to throw the boys into the furnace in the first place were then themselves thrown in there. And, this time, they perished due to flames and sparks.

Taking Our Eyes Off God

I now know that many times in my life, by operating in fear, I took my eyes off of God and focused upon my circumstances. This reminds me of the story in the Bible in which Jesus was walking on the water, and

Peter saw him walking on the water (doing a miraculous thing). Peter said to him, "If that is really you, tell me to come to you on the water." (Essentially, Peter wanted to do the same thing Jesus was doing). So Jesus said, "Well, come on." Peter got out of the boat and began walking on the water towards Jesus. It wasn't until he took his eyes off of Jesus and looked at his circumstances — that he was actually walking on water too — that he experienced fear and then immediately Peter began to sink.

Why did he begin to sink? It's because he switched his focus. Peter experienced fear by focusing on his circumstances, not on God. Jesus did not fail Peter. Peter failed Peter because he was walking, albeit on water, and then he began to fear.

I identify so very much with Peter. There have been times when I was doing miraculous, supernatural things, and whenever I took my eyes off of Jesus, I began to "sink" back to my mortal self with less power and more fear. I climbed back "in the boat" where I was comfortable because my faith wasn't strong enough. I was focused on what others would think of me, walking on water and all. But then I realized that even if I were walking on water, the "haters" would say it was because I couldn't swim.

Don't be afraid to say what needs to be said to make a difference in your life or the life of another person. You see, there will be people who you cannot please no matter what. Therefore, keep focused, and since you're walking on water, you might as well dance on it. Because the thing about God is that, He won't let us rest in mediocrity. He created us with seeds of greatness inside. Now it's up to us to create the environment for the seeds to germinate.

An environment where fear exists will not allow the seeds of greatness to grow and develop. If we ignore this fact, and we suffer from fear, we will often find ourselves in a "sink or walk on water" situation. At that point, we are then forced to make a choice. I find those times to be extremely uncomfortable, and so I work on my faith muscle to keep fear at bay. Fear and faith cannot exist in the same place. So if I focus and feed my faith, then the fear dissipates and eventually dies of starvation.

*"The greatest mistake you can make in life
is to be continually fearing you will make one."*
~ Elbert Hubbard

Choosing Our Response to Fear
I know that you think that you feel fear. It seems tangible. But how much should we truly trust our feelings? Especially when we have self-imposed them through inviting fear in. I heard someone say, "Feelings are a lot like waves, we can't stop them from coming, but we can decide which ones to surf." I love that because I now realize that I have the power to act or ride on the wave of fear when it comes my way, or I can choose to let it pass and wait for a better, more positive wave to come along.

Be Uncompromisingly Optimistic

"A pessimist finds the darkness around the light but an optimist becomes the light in the darkness."
~ Debasish Mridha

As the reigning Queen of Optimism, I find that people often ask me what it really means to be optimistic. Do you optimistic ones ever have bad days? Are you always so darn happy? These are common misconceptions about optimists. Let me first clear some things up right off the bat.

A Special Way of Seeing

Life happens to optimistic people too. It's just about putting things in their proper perspective that makes the difference for us. As we often discuss here, an optimist recognizes that it is never what it looks like. While we do have challenges and life often presents its gifts of growth for us to open up, we "see" what others don't see. We have the special ability to change the way we look at things. If there is any attribute that is most critical to living a successful life, it is that one.

Show me successful people from the most widely selected walks of life — be it success in career, business, family or personal life — and I'll show you, optimists. It's virtually impossible to be successful and not be optimistic. Only what you can "see" will be objectified in your world. Pick one, any one, of these successful people and I can guarantee that this person had to, at some point, change the way they were looking at things in order to accomplish the task or goal that ensured their success.

Optimists do and try things that others think are crazy. They seem to always find a way where there was not previously a way. We simply see what others don't see. We walk by faith and not by sight.

Optimists also have vision. Vision is the ability to see things as they

could be, not just as they are right now. That is how we can see the glass not just half-full but overflowing. It takes real heart to have a vision. You undeniably take a chance on people thinking you're crazy when you share your vision with others. But don't worry… you will be shown to be right in the end. Stick with it. Be uncompromising in your optimism. Let no one take it from you.

It takes vision to see the potential that lies within an entire human life — your own human life. Some people are rather good at that while some are not. Vision is not a function of the eyes. One does not need sight to have vision. I know some blind people who have more vision than most people with fully functioning eyesight. With vision, you are acting on things that are not immediately visible. Vision needs a visionary to make it come to pass. That visionary should be you.

Now I must also clear up another misconception. People often confuse being optimistic with thinking positive. Being an optimist and living your life that way is far beyond just positive thinking. Like with the optimists I describe above, it's about how you "see" your world and everything (and everyone) in it. Remember, we don't see things as they are, we see things as we are. You can actually "look" at a situation but not really "see" it for what it really is. An optimist can take a more introspective look and see something different than what it looks like. While the search is with a positive lens, it is far beyond that.

Making the conscious choice to live my life optimistic has been the best decision I've ever made. I raise my children that way, approach my relationships that way, my career, my businesses, etc. I am uncompromisingly optimistic and proud of it.

There are many advantages. Studies have proven that optimistic people live longer, healthier lives, make more money, have better sex, and raise more successful, happier, brighter children. Optimism allows you to approach difficulty with strength and resolve. It decreases anxiety, frustration and worries.

Optimistic people are more productive, more valued members of society. Our optimism is one of the most precious natural resources we have, and it must be protected and nurtured.

I Only Hire Optimists

If you choose this lifestyle, you must refuse to listen to pessimistic people. Don't let people pull you into their world and insult you with their pessimism without your permission.

I'm laughing as I write this piece because I can't tell you how many professional people have lost out on my business because they were pessimistic. When I was looking for a lawyer a few years back to handle a business matter, I interviewed ten different attorneys before I found one who was optimistic. All the others gave me the grim "gloom and doom" scenario, and they were critical of my optimism. How could I feel confident in their abilities when they told me that I could never win the case?

I kept it moving until I found an attorney who was at least trying to be optimistic. I can tell you, though, an optimistic attorney is not that easy to find! I get that you have to present the facts to your client. However, there's nothing wrong with being optimistic about the outcome, especially when the client is in the right. Just as a side note, optimism did prevail and I won the case because my attorney relied upon my optimism and his talent to believe justice would prevail. He now tells me how much better of a lawyer he is because of his change in perspective.

The same goes for doctors, teachers and coaches or, for that matter, any person who expects to get my business or work with me and or my family. A pessimistic approach will never get my money or attention. If you don't feel positive or optimistic about the situation, no matter how it "looks," we will not work together. I can't afford it.

> *"So we don't look at the troubles we can see now;*
> *rather, we fix our gaze on things that cannot be seen.*
> *For the things we see now will soon be gone,*
> *but the things we cannot see will last forever."*
> ~ 2 Corinthians 4:18

Not Always the Easy Path

Consider the Story of Viktor Frankl as a true example of an optimist. Viktor witnessed the senseless killings of his father, mother, brother and loving wife in the concentration camps of Nazi Germany. He lost everything, including a compilation of his life's work that he was forced to surrender over to his captives at Auschwitz. In spite of, or perhaps because of, all of that, Viktor emerged an optimist. Not just any optimist, his most famous book, *Man's Search for Meaning*, has gone on to become one of the top 10 most influential books of all time, according to the Library of Congress. Over 9 million copies and counting have been sold, and even after Viktor Frankl has transitioned, he still inspires us all.

It has personally not been easy wearing the crown as The Queen of Optimism. Somehow, people think that an optimist doesn't experience challenges and pain. That's not the point. As I noted earlier in the chapter, the point is how we choose to "see" the world we live in and what we believe those things we "see" mean for our own lives and for those we love. Therein is the choice. We have the choice to believe what we see or to believe the unseen. What you see as a problem, I may see as an opportunity. You may hear the word "no" and think it's the end, while I may hear the word "no" and think that person just doesn't have enough information yet to get to a "yes." I am optimistic and unapologetic about that.

I have been given the awesome job of sharing the optimistic advantage with others, and so I must never give up. I am charged with telling you the truth — unashamed and unabashed. There may be physical evidence of darkness all around, but I am looking to the light. I carry it with me, and I know you carry it with you also.

So I am not giving up. How can I? Even though on the outside it looks like things are falling apart on us, on the inside, where God is making new life, not a day goes by without his unfolding grace and love. These hard times are small potatoes compared to the coming good times, the lavish celebration prepared for us. There is far more here than meets the (naked) eye. The things we see now are here today, gone tomorrow. But the things we can't see will last forever. That's what I believe. I am confident that the best is yet to come.

Watch Your Mouth

"For one word a man is often deemed to be wise,
and for one word he is often deemed to be foolish.
We should indeed be careful what we say."
~ Confucius

The power of the written and spoken word is not a new phenomenon. In ancient Mesopotamia, some of the most powerful individuals were scribes. They were the only ones with the ability to write and read cuneiform, the first written language. Scribes controlled the word, so they had the power to control the people.

Words equal power, and you can use them for good or evil. I know what you're thinking. It's probably something like "Why didn't everyone just learn to read and write in cuneiform?" Not so fast... the people believed that scribes were chosen by the Gods. It was such an important piece of their society that they believed the Gods were the only ones capable of choosing who could be a keeper of the word. So, at that time, only certain people could be in possession of the word. Do we consider the things we say and write as important as the ancient Mesopotamians did? Perhaps we should.

"What goes into a man's mouth does not make him 'unclean,'
but what comes out of his mouth, that is what makes him 'unclean.'"
~ Matthew 15:10

According to King Solomon, life and death are in the power of the tongue. The Greek playwright Euripides went on to affirm that every unbridled tongue in the end shall find itself unfortunate. An unbridled tongue is one which has no control or restraint. The Book of James,

Chapter 3, verses 3-12 goes in-depth about the power of the tongue, and it gives us the framework for this chapter.

Small, But Extremely Powerful

If you can control your tongue, you can control your body and your circumstances. Although the tongue is one of the smallest parts of our body, it is arguable the most powerful to our very existence.

We put bits in a horse's mouth; thus we can control the entire body of a huge horse with only this small bit. Unfortunately, we don't have bits in our mouths that could control our whole body. However, we should quickly find a way to tame that part of us.

Our tongue is compared to kindleth because it can start great fires. A kindleth or kindle is something that starts a fire or lights a torch. Whenever I want to start a fire in our fireplace in the family room, we go outside and get some logs that were cut down from a tree in the backyard. We gather the logs and stack them up and try to light them. Nothing really happens until we add that small starter log, or kindleth, to the pile of large logs. Soon thereafter we will have a good fire going.

That starter log is the size of a tiny brick. It is a fraction of the size of just one of those logs, but it really gets the fire blazing. So goes your tongue. Although it's small, it is extremely powerful — just like that starter log — and it can really start a huge blaze.

Loose Lips Sink Lives

To emphasize the power of the tongue, let us turn again to the Bible. In Chapter 3 of the Book of James, the Bible also compares the tongue to a rudder of a ship. A rudder is a device used to steer a ship, boat, submarine, hovercraft, aircraft or other conveyance that moves through a medium — generally air or water. The rudder is also small in comparison to the vessel that it controls, yet it can steer a large vessel in any direction — either into or out of a storm.

"Don't make your words too salty,
you may have to go back and eat them later."
~ Shelley Roxanne

Have you ever met people who are either unwilling or unable to control their tongue? Look at their lives and you will see destruction everywhere. They have what some call "loose lips" and just say whatever comes to their mind. Well, it has often been said that "loose lips sink ships."

This phrase was coined as a slogan during WWII as part of the US Office of War Information's attempt to limit the possibility of people inadvertently giving useful information to enemy spies. The slogan was actually "Loose Lips Might Sink Ships." This was one of several similar slogans that all came under the campaign's basic message, "Careless Talk Costs Lives." Careless talk does cost lives; it could cost you your life. Your success or failure in life is directly tied to your ability to bridle your tongue.

It is written... "that every careless word that people speak, they shall give an accounting for it on the Day of Judgment."
~ Matthew 12:36

In Proverbs, it tells us that if we have a bad thought, we are to put our hand over our mouth, because once it comes out of your mouth, you will see it come into your life. That is how powerful words are.

Sticks and stones may break my bones, but words will never harm me. Who said that? It is so untrue. Remember, as a child, we were taught to make that statement when someone said something mean to us. You know what I'm talking about. The bully who said mean things to you in the playground or lunchroom. Anyway, whoever said words can't harm was wrong. Words are the most powerful tools in the universe.

Hey, the Bible even tells us that "in the beginning was the Word." Words, when well chosen, have so great a force in them that they can create life or take it away.

When my son was in elementary school, he came home telling his grandmother and me that a bully was calling him names. We asked him if he identified with what he was being called by the bully. And he confirmed that he did not. "Then don't let it hurt your feelings," said his grandmother. "How can it not?" he answered back.

That one hit me really hard because I knew exactly what he meant. I realize that the right and logical thing as a responsible parent would be to tell a seven-year-old child not to let it affect him. But how can it not? Instead, what I did was just held him tightly and attempted to quickly erase that negative programming from his computer (subconscious). People have said things to or about me that were not supposed to hurt my feelings. And, as my son said, how can it not?

"It is with words as with sunbeams...
the more they are condensed, the deeper they burn."
~ Robert Southey

Don't Call Dead What You Want Alive
This story is of a Shunammite woman found in II Kings 4:8-37. She was an influential wealthy woman in town. She met a traveling prophet named Elisha and saw he was a great man of God.

Being a generous person, this woman fed the traveling prophet and even offered him a place to stay in her home each time he was in town. She was so thoughtful and generous that she eventually had her husband build an addition onto their house for Elisha to stay. The prophet was grateful to the woman for her generosity and wondered what he could do for her as an expression of his gratitude.

Elisha saw that although this woman seemingly had everything material in her life, she did not have a child. So, he spoke a word to her that within one year she would give birth to a son. Sure enough, within that same year, just as the prophet spoke, the woman gave birth to her son. Years past and the boy grew. One day her son was working out in the field with his father when he complained about a pain in his head. The father had the son carried inside to his mother where later died in his mother's arms.

The Shunammite woman took her son's lifeless body upstairs to the prophet Elisha's room and laid him on the prophets bed, and she shut the door. The woman, without saying a word, got dressed, putting on her Sunday best clothes. She told her husband; I will be right back, All is well. She drove to the place where the prophet Elisha was speaking to a crowd of followers. He saw her in the distance and upon greeting her, asked her how was everyone in the family. Your husband? Your son? And her response was...All is well.

All is well was her response. Now this woman's son is "dead" and laying lifeless at her house, and she is there telling the prophet that All is well. The prophet goes back to the house with the woman finding the boy dead on his bed. He went into his bedroom, shut the door on the two of them, and he prayed to the Lord. He stretched himself upon the child, and the child sneezed and opened his eyes. He came alive again.

Because of her faith and because of her words, the woman's son was brought back to life. She could have spoken death to her situation. Frankly, she would have only been speaking facts. It was a fact that her son was lifeless and without a pulse. She could have panicked and told her husband that their precious son was dead, but instead she chose to speak life to the matter. Instead, she said All is well. The facts didn't count for this woman. She called those things that were not as though they were.

Words were spoken to bring her son back to life and to make it all well - just as she said. The only thing unusual about this woman was her faith. She had great faith. But as for the power of words, she simply used what is available to all of us. Life and death are in the power of your tongue as well.

Words Have Lasting Effects

Words can make people healthy, words can involve people in million dollar libel suits, words can degrade character and convict criminals. Therefore, it's important to improve your speech. Many people have been held captive in their circumstances by their own words. Well, they do say, "You live by the sword and die by the sword." Your words, my friend, are the sword.

Have you ever seen a court proceeding where the lawyer is giving his summation, and he makes accusations against the defendant that are out of line and defaming? The judge tells the jury to strike it from the record. Come on now, how can they do that? The jury already heard the words spoken. They have already been released into the atmosphere and cannot be taken back. A good prosecuting attorney knows this all too well and will use it if he has to in order to win. Sure, the court reporter can document that it was stricken from the recorded written record, but you cannot strike it from your mental record as easily.

Have you ever, in the heat of an argument, said something that you later apologized for by saying something like "I did not mean that, I'm sorry." That person can forgive you and perhaps attempt to strike it from the record, but its sting has lasting effects that are not easily forgotten.

This reminds me of a story of the young boy who had a bad temper. His father gave him a bag of nails and told him that every time he lost his temper, he must hammer a nail into the back of the fence. The first day the boy had driven 37 nails into the fence. Over the next few weeks, as he learned to control his anger, the number of nails hammered daily gradually dwindled down. The boy discovered that it was easier to hold his temper than to drive those nails into the fence.

Finally, the day came when the boy didn't lose his temper at all. He told his father about it, and the father suggested that the boy now pull out one nail for each day that he was able to hold his temper. The days passed and the young boy was finally able to tell his father that all the nails were gone. The father took his son by the hand and led him to the fence. He said, "You have done well, my son, but look at the holes in the fence. The fence will never be the same.

When you say things in anger, they leave a scar just like this one. You can put a knife in a man and draw it out. It won't matter how many times you say I'm sorry, the wound is still there. A verbal wound is as bad as or perhaps even worse than a physical one."

One of the most important things we choose to use every day that we can't get back is our words. If just for today you treated your words like money, would you choose to spend them the way you have been spending them? If all else fails, you always have the right to remain silent. Do that.

Give Thanks

"Happiness cannot be traveled to, owned, earned, worn or consumed. Happiness is the spiritual experience of living every minute with love, grace, and gratitude."
~ Denis Waitley

Each day should be a day of thanksgiving. Don't reserve this expression of gratitude for one day a year — the fourth Thursday in November. Giving thanks should be something we do every day. Be sure to make the words "thank you" a standard in your vocabulary.

It's amazing how powerful those two little words can be. Offering gratitude for things and people actually brings more of that thing into your life. Saying thank you is more than just good manners; it is so much more.

As long as you have a grateful heart, you will always find reasons to be grateful. Gratitude is an integral part of success is one's life. The scriptures are filled with passages urging us to give thanks for the gifts that have been bestowed upon us.

Nothing new or good can come into your life without gratitude.

Keeping a gratitude journal is very helpful for most people. That way, whenever you're feeling down, you can check back in your gratitude journal and review everything you listed previously that you are grateful for.

Being Grateful at a Challenging Time

We should be eternally grateful not for just the obvious, but also for our thousands of fortunate moments and our multitude of blessings. Even be grateful for the hard times. Without challenges, there would be no progress. Without obstacles, there can be no achievement. Be thankful for the opportunities that they provide.

Looking straight into the face of adversity and being grateful can produce amazing, long-lasting blessings. When my son was very young, he had a medical condition that required surgery. Although it was told to us that the surgery was minor, no surgery is minor especially for your baby. In the midst of that period, I felt grateful. I was grateful to have had the one-on-one time to pray with him, to love on him, to shower him with gifts and attention.

Ironically, this occurred during a time when I sensed that my son was feeling the squeeze of being a middle child. In the rush of life raising three boys and having a busy lifestyle, sometimes it's hard to stop and smell the roses. Although I did not want my baby to have to experience these circumstances, I decided to be grateful for the gifts that were given to us —including more time together. I truly believe that after that experience, he never again questioned his place in our lives nor questioned the love that his family and friends have for him. For that, he and I are eternally grateful.

"Gratitude can turn negatives into positives. Find a way to be thankful for your adversities and they can become your blessings."
~ Shelley Roxanne

Thanks-giving at a Time of Loss
I remember when Glo, my mom, passed away. The very first thing I felt — well, honestly, not the very first thing but one of the first — was gratitude. I was overwhelmed with thanks-giving for being blessed with the most awesome mother in all the world. It was at that moment that I knew for sure that life is real, that time is short, that you never know when someone you love will transition.

Now I practice gratitude and showing and demonstrating love to those I care about because you truly never know. Applying gratitude and love to that very traumatic situation helped me to deal with it. I was grateful for all the laughs we shared, which were many. I was grateful for all the tears we cried, which were few. I was grateful for the love we shared, which was tremendous.

When I would do things for her, Glo used to say, "Until I am able to better pay you, thank you is all I can give you for now." Well, that was always enough for me.

> *"The deepest craving of human nature*
> *is the need to be appreciated."*
> ~ William James

I celebrated Glo's life on her birthday, which was about a month after her transition, to give myself and others an opportunity to express gratitude for the joy she brought to our lives. Since Glo was a lover of the casinos, I threw her a casino-themed party. I had a Broadway sign company make a gigantic sign with her name in lights. As centerpieces, we had all of her favorite things displayed for people to enjoy.

As the party favor, I gave away personal items of hers as a token of gratitude for the people who came out to celebrate Glo's life. I often run into people wearing her scarf, brooch or bracelet, or carrying one of her purses, and they tell me they wear it when they need a "Glo pick-me-up." I'm constantly moved by the people who appreciated the joy that Glo brought to their lives and the bright light that she had.

Other Different Takes on Gratitude

There is so much to be grateful for that you may take for granted.

I still count my babies' ages by months. It may sound weird when someone asks me how old my children are, and I tell them, the oldest is 336 months, my middle one is 228 months, and the baby is 192 months old. I never understood why it was OK to count months when they were babies but once they reach the age of two, we already start the rounding down the process. That's OK if they look at me strangely. I am grateful for each month.

Apply gratitude to even the very things you desire. If you consistently apply gratitude for already receiving those desires, they must manifest in your life. This too is a spiritual law. Expressing deep and profound gratitude is critical to your success. The more grateful you are, the more things you will have to be grateful for.

Be grateful even for not enough. After all, you get more of what you're grateful for. Gratitude can multiply and make not enough more than enough. What you're grateful for expands.

I am reminded about the story in the Gospel of John about how Jesus fed 5,000 men, not counting the women and children (easily about 20,000 people in total), with only five barley loaves and two fish. For the Bible scholars out there or if you have ever been to Sunday school or church ever in your life, I know you have heard this story.

This miracle often referred to as "feeding the multitude," is present in all four canonical gospels — Matthew, Mark, Luke, and John. The disciples who hung with Jesus at that time all tell the story, and although each account may slightly differ in minor details, there is one thing they all agreed that happened — which I believe to be a pivotal point in this miracle. This was the fact that Jesus was presented with the dilemma of having to feed tens of thousands of people by sharing a little boy's lunch. The very first thing he did was to give thanks for the little he had to work with.

After Jesus had given thanks for the little that was in his hand, it became enough to feed everyone. Once all the people ate until they were full, the disciples gathered up the leftovers and filled twelve baskets with the fragments left by those who then had more than enough to eat.

How many times have we been confronted in our lives with situations where we needed to take care of something but by appearances what we had was not enough? I know I've been there more times than I'd like to remember.

Nonetheless, I also know that in those times when I was grateful for the little I did have, somehow it became more than enough for me to accomplish the task at hand.

> *"When you are grateful,*
> *fear disappears, and abundance appears."*
> ~ Anthony Robbins

Teaching Gratitude to Our Children
When you think about it, "thank you" is usually among the first phrases

we teach to our children as toddlers. There are no greater words you can hear a little two-year-old say than "thank you." It sounds so sweet and special. Well, it sounds just as good when they are 22, 32, 42 or 72.

Have your children frequently articulated out loud what they are grateful for? During Thanksgiving every year, my grandmother, Nana, would have us go around the table to state what we were grateful for. That was such a special time for our family. I now have adopted that with my own children, and I am always amazed at the beautiful things I hear that come from them. I actually learn so much about them and what is in their hearts when they articulate what they are grateful for.

Thankfully my boys happen to be very grateful people. Each and every night that I cook dinner, they get up from the table and say, "Thank you for dinner, Mommy." Each and every time I hear that, my heart jumps with joy. I know how special and joyful their lives will be in the future because they live with grateful hearts.

Thanking People in Advance

There are so many ways to express gratitude, be it a handwritten note, flowers, a book that helped you that you've already read, a CD that inspired you, etc. Whether it's a teacher, staff or the delivery guy (anyone who provides you a service), you should show your gratitude. It comes back in big ways.

When the boys were in grade school, on the first day of school I would send the teacher a "thank you" gift (saying a grace of sorts). I usually gave them a box of chocolate with a note that said something like "Today I present you with two gifts, this chocolate, and my son. Enjoy them both and thank you in advance for a great school experience."

The note was not a bribe. It was a sincere gesture to let the teacher know that I appreciated the fact that they were going to impart knowledge to my child and for that I was grateful in anticipation for a great school year. Invariably, they later shared with me how much of a gift my son had been to them and how much they appreciated all the gift(s) I shared with them that school year.

On a related note, researchers have actually proven that showing gratitude can increase business. A jewelry store found that customers who were called and thanked for making a purchase were 70% more likely to return and purchase more. Restaurateurs found that when the server writes the words "thank you" on the check, that server is much more likely to get a larger tip. It pays to give thanks.

There are other benefits to gratitude. For instance, if you want more joy in your life, be grateful. It is not joy that makes us grateful. It is gratitude that makes us joyful. Studies have also found that people who are grateful have better mental health. Grateful people experience less sickness and depression, and they are more forgiving, happier people.

A Daily Practice

Practice gratitude each day. Spread gratitude like a lotion. Apply it generously to every situation and circumstance and you will see that situation turn around. There is magic in the ointment called gratitude.

Before heading into a meeting, I give thanks. Before I go on the air, I give thanks. Before my children begin their sporting events, I give thanks. Before I sit down to write, I give thanks. I give thanks because I am grateful for what is about to happen. I am grateful for being put into a situation to enjoy what I am about to experience.

Saying grace does not have to be, nor should it be simply something we say before we are about to eat a meal. It should be a way of life.

When making gratitude a practice, you may be surprised to find how drastically your life can change. When giving thanks and showing gratitude for all the things in your life, you will demonstrate the ancient spiritual law which states, "The more you have and are grateful for, the more will be given you."

Thank you for reading this book. I appreciate you.

Don't Worry, All Is Well

"It's not time to worry yet."
~ Harper Lee, *To Kill a Mockingbird*

Who by worrying can add a single hour to their life? Let's face it… worry is as useless as a handle on a snowball. It's the interest paid in advance on a debt you may never owe. Frankly, if your problem has a solution, then why worry about it? If your problem doesn't have a solution, then why worry about it? Worrying makes no sense, and it has absolutely no beneficial qualities whatsoever. I should know since I was once a "professional worrier." If there were a competition, I would have received the Gold Medal in Worry. Part of it came from being a perfectionist Virgo and the other part came through heredity.

Closet Worriers

My family members were basically closet worriers. We didn't worry in public, nor did we express our worry to others in private. That was not proper. We only worried in the privacy of our own minds. It was there that Worry set up house — right in our own heads. Worry had furniture, hung chandeliers and even had parties. To these parties, it always invited Fear — its first and closest cousin. In fact, Worry and Fear went everywhere together. You see, when you let one of them in, it brings its relatives along — Worry, Fear, Doubt, Anxiety and the rest of the clan.

I should have charged them rent for the space they took up in my head for all those years. Yes, it took me years to figure out that Worry was simply a cheap substitute for Faith. Sitting around thinking over and over again about what you don't want to happen is like doing a dress

rehearsal for when it does. Stop rehearsing for hurts and failure that may never even come. That is not Faith. That is Doubt, and it robs you of a great life.

Here's the thing. Whatever is going to happen will happen anyway, whether or not you worry about it — so what's the point? Worry doesn't stop a future event from happening, so it's not a good investment of your time.

On top of that, worrying seems to give small things a very big shadow. It seems that, by worrying, you put that issue under a magnifying glass and enhance its negative properties even more. Surely that makes no sense, does it?

It's Not Time to Worry Yet

Frankly it is never a good time to worry. I find that most believers worry about money. Somehow they are under the misconception that they don't have enough to accomplish their tasks or goals. All I can tell you about this is that those who trust in the Lord will never lack any good thing. You have everything you need for the season you are in right now. If you don't have it right now, than you don't need it right now. So why worry?

The past is gone, and the future is not here as yet, so all we have is now. Truly, today is our most treasured possession. So release your attachment to worrying about tomorrow. When we worry, we miss the present.

Worry is also addictive. Plus, it's the kind of addiction that you can pass on to your children. They learn to worry and become afraid because you worry and are afraid.

Worry destroys our ability to concentrate. It makes you tense and nervous. When we worry, we are not at peace. Worry also has physical impacts. The human body is not meant to live in the state of chaos that worry can create. Worry can, therefore, contribute to ailments such as high blood pressure, heart attacks, stomach problems, cancer, and depression.

Most worry is caused by confusion or a lack of knowledge. Most times when you have the facts, you'll find that you don't have anything to worry about after all. I know people actually believe that worry somehow prepares you for the inevitable event, but this is a deception.

Most things that cause us worry are not based upon truth but are based on speculation, conjecture, rumor and bad information.

> *"Take no thought (do not worry) for tomorrow.*
> *Tomorrow will care for itself."*
> ~ Matthew 6:34

A Worried Mom
When my son Myles was a baby, I nursed him for 18 months. When I was ready to wean him from breastfeeding, I was told that I needed to go away for at least five days and that I could not be in the same house with him. I did as I was instructed, kissed my baby — who by this time was walking, talking and laughing — and got on a flight to Texas to visit my girlfriend, Marcia. She had set up shopping excursions and other fun events (all involved eating, of course) for while I was in town.

Instead of enjoying myself on my vacation, I worried the entire time that Myles wouldn't eat, that he would never forgive me for leaving him like that, etc., etc. I worried that he would starve waiting for me to return. I spent the entire trip in bed going through a physical and mental withdrawal, added on top with a big 'ole dose of guilt and worry.

Upon my return, I couldn't wait to see my baby. I expected him to run to me in excitement when I came through the door. Instead, he laid on the floor motionless. I motioned for him to walk to me, but he wouldn't come. I went to pick him up and stand him on his feet, but he just fell to the ground. My baby couldn't walk!

Oh my goodness, what have I done? I thought. Have I destroyed my child for life? I took him to a series of doctor's appointments to determine what was wrong. Did he lose his ability to walk because I had stopped breastfeeding him? I know that sounds crazy, but nobody said worrying had to make sense.

I worried for three whole weeks with every possible scenario going through my mind from extreme to more extreme. In the end, when I finally relaxed and evicted Worry and its family from my head, Myles got off of a doctor's table and walked out of the office. Apparently all he had was a simple cold in his hip. He was fine, and I was relieved. But I had

lost an entire month of my life. I couldn't sleep, eat or be joyful because I was uselessly worrying.

"Don't be anxious (worry) about anything."
~ Philippians 4:6

A Simple 3-Step Process

Only you can free yourself from the self-imposed prison that worry creates. You hold the key, so don't waste another moment in fear and worry.

Here is a three-step process that you can use to defeat worry:

Step 1. Ask yourself, "What's the worst that can happen?"
Step 2. Accept that.
Step 3. Calmly proceed to improve upon the worst thing to the best of your ability… then Pray and don't worry about it again.

" There are very few monsters
who warrant the fear we have of them."
~ Andre Gide

In the end, all is well… so if all is not well right now, it's not the end. Just hold on, things will work out fine.

Laugh More

"Laughter is the shortest distance
between two people."
~ Victor Borge

Laughing is probably one of my favorite activities. I just plain love to laugh. I must have gotten that from my mother. This woman laughed up until the very last day. As a matter of fact, the last night I saw Glo, we were laughing about something we had seen or heard that day.

Laughter binds us together, lightens our burdens, and assists us in keeping things in perspective. We can all use a little attitudinal adjustment from time to time. Laughter helps to do just that. Researchers say happy people are healthy people. It's written that a cheerful heart is good medicine.

Finding humor even in difficult situations can be a very powerful practice. If you can manage to find humor during trying times you win. You take the wind out of the sail of your opposition and don't allow it to steal your joy. It is written that the joy of the Lord is your strength. You can outsmart the enemy simply by maintaining a happy countenance.

"Some cause happiness wherever they go; others, whenever they go."
-Oscar Wilde

Lighten-Up
It's often that we simply take ourselves too seriously when we need to just lighten up. I spearheaded a campaign I called Lighten Up America in which I sought to travel the country finding the happiest people in the nation. I was surprised to find that it was not the people with the

107

most money that were smiling and happy, but it was the people who put things in their proper perspective. They were - dare I say it - optimistic. It appears that optimistic people were happy people, and happy people were optimistic people. When I make the case to coaching clients about why they should want to be more optimistic, especially the men, I simply tell them that optimistic people have better sex lives because they can see small things big and big things small. That usually does it for them.

A Laugh a Day Keeps Doc Away

According to a recent study, laughter, along with an active sense of humor, may help protect you against a heart attack. The study, which is the first to indicate that laughter may help prevent heart disease, found that people with heart disease were 40 percent less likely to laugh in a variety of situations compared to people of the same age without heart disease.

Although they don't quite know exactly how the laughter protects the heart, they do know that mental stress is associated with impairment of the endothelium, the protective barrier lining our blood vessels. This can cause a series of inflammatory reactions that lead to fat and cholesterol build-up in the coronary arteries and ultimately to a heart attack.

Laughter is also attributed to lowering blood pressure, increasing muscle flexion, and boosting our immune system. Besides all that, it is downright fun. Turns out a hearty laugh a day keeps the doctor away. Physicians who are aware that laughter is the best medicine are now prescribing it to their patients. Along with recommending exercise and eating right, they're telling their patients to laugh a few times a day.

> *Laughter is a tranquilizer with no side effects.*
> - Arnold Glasgow

I heard a story of a woman who was diagnosed with breast cancer. She spent the next 30 days laughing at comedies and funny things. She went back to the doctor after her comedy treatment, and the cancerous tumor was gone.

Get Your Laughter Workout In
I have more good news; they say that laughing is like working out from the inside. While researching the benefits of laughter, I found a study by the American College of Cardiology that reported that provoking laughter did as much good for the arteries as aerobic activity. Isn't that good news for those of us who do not enjoy working out in the traditional sense?

Now let me be honest, the study does not recommend you laugh and not exercise. However, it does suggest the benefits of laughter are good for the vascular system. One pioneer in laughter research claimed it took 10 minutes on a rowing machine for his heart rate to reach the level it would after just one minute of hearty laughter. Just laugh your way to a better body. Ha, Ha, Ha.

"Nothing feels as good to me as laughing incredibly hard. "
- Steve Carell

Join the Laughter Movement
Laughter is seen as so important in today's culture that there is a Laughter Movement going on around the world. This merry movement is holding laughter events all across Europe, Asia, South America and The United States. The leaders of this movement believe that everyone in the world should take time to relax and lighten up. Studies show that children laugh 400 times a day while adults only laugh 15 times per day. What do they know that we don't? There's no greater sound than the sound of a laughing child.

I love to hear anyone laugh. I don't know about you but it makes me happy to hear other people laughing and it's contagious. Now, that's something I don't mind catching. Not only do I love to laugh, but I also love to make other people laugh as well. Perhaps in another life I would have been a comedian and to some degree I already am. Every chance I get, I will go to a comedy show or put on a movie that, although I may have seen it hundreds of times, still makes me laugh.

"Mix a little foolishness with your serious plans. It is lovely to be silly at the right moment."
- Horace

Be Silly

I am hands down the silliest person in my house. Truth be told I am the silliest person I know. There is a good reason for that. It begins with that fact that I refuse to take myself or anyone else too seriously. Because of the fact that I know that it's never what it looks like, I can laugh at situations that appear adverse. I have too much proof and evidence that all things work out for my good eventually, so I am going to keep it light and silly.

One of the greatest qualities about my father, besides that handsome and charming smile, is his sense of humor. I admired his ability to make us laugh even when things didn't seem so funny. He found humor in it. It made all the difference in the world to me.

"You cannot climb the ladder of success dressed in the costume of failure."
- Zig Ziglar

Put on Your Costume

Sometimes we just need to put on our super hero capes and conquer our circumstances. In our family, we loved Halloween. Not for the creepy, gruesomeness but because it was a chance to dress up and become something else, something you always wanted to be. Each year I would let the boys choose their costume, and I would go to great lengths to make it happen for them. I even once traveled to New York City where the costume designers shop for costumes for Broadway plays, to rent a costume for Evan because authenticity was important in our dress up.

When Myles was about 18 months old, he chose the character Buzz Lightyear, from the Toy Story movies as his costume. A few days before Halloween that year, we let him try on his costume for fit. It looked amazing. It had the muscles built in, although even then Myles didn't need the padding since he was "swole" even as a baby. It had the boots

and the wrist devices so that you could speak to "command center" and, of course, it came equipped with the Jet Pack. The Jet Pack had wings that you pop out just before you are about to take flight. Just after Jeff and I dressed Myles in his costume, he climbed up on our high platformed bed, put his hands on his hips, declared that he was about to fly to infinity and beyond...and he leaped. Luckily, Jeff was right there to catch him or the few teeth Myles did have at the time would probably have been knocked out by a pretty nasty fall. But it taught me something.

Sometimes, we have to play dress up and put on a costume in order to feel powerful and invincible. And that's OK. We may have to fake it 'till we make it. Dress for the job you want, not the job you have. If necessary, create an alter ego, if you don't yet feel confident in presenting yourself the way you truly want to be. Why not? Beyonce has Sasha Fierce; Kobe Bryant has Black Mamba, and Myles had Buzz Lightyear. Maybe you too can travel to infinity and beyond if you just put your cape on and leap.

Practice the F Word
(Forgiveness)

*"If you want to see brave,
look at those who can forgive."*
~ Bhagavad Gita

Forgiveness is the Law of Release. It is for our benefit. Ultimately it is the gift we give ourselves. Be quick to give forgiveness. When you forgive, you release. Un-forgiveness causes you to harbor the sin of someone else in your life.

Un-forgiveness is a form of self-abuse. I heard it said that harboring un-forgiveness is like taking poison and hoping the other person dies. Now that sounds pretty crazy to me. Doesn't it sound ridiculous to you? If you want to be free, know that true freedom means you're walking with a clear conscious. The best sleep you can get is sleeping on a soft, clear conscious.

Don't forget, while you're practicing the art of forgiveness, to forgive the most important person - YOU. You must forgive yourself. This frees you from the self-imposed prison that guilt and shame create.

*"The weak can never forgive.
Forgiveness is the attribute of the strong."*
~ Mahatma Gandhi

No Confrontation Needed
Forgiving someone else doesn't mean you have to have a confrontation or meeting of the minds with them. You can even forgive someone who is dead. It's something you do within yourself. You are releasing that person and yourself from any further bondage. Even if you don't think they deserve it, you surely do.

Most often someone who has wronged or offended you has moved on to their other victims and has long forgotten about you. Meanwhile, you are walking around stuck, angry and hurt. Release it immediately and go on about the business of living.

> *"There is no revenge so complete as forgiveness."*
> ~ Josh Billings

Forgiving the Seemingly Unforgivable

Immaculee Ilibagiza's story is the most astounding example of forgiveness. Immaculee is a survivor of the 1994 genocide in Rwanda, Africa. Her story is moving and remarkable. You can read all about it in her best-selling book, *Left to Tell.*

One of the most remarkable parts of her story is the fact that most of Immaculee's family was savagely murdered as she hid in a small bathroom. There she remained for 91 days with seven other women hiding from certain death. After more than three months of hiding, unable to speak, bathe, or eat, she was freed from that three-foot by four-foot prison. She entered that tiny bathroom as a healthy 125-pound woman and exited as a 65-pound skeleton.

Immaculee tells the poignant story of one of history's bloodiest holocausts with such passion and love. Her story so compelled me that I decided to interview her on my Radio Show. Throughout the entire interview, all I kept wondering was how in the world could she forgive these people for what they did to her. She experienced something most people could not even imagine and yet the first thing she did when released from that bathroom was going about the act of forgiving.

I asked her, "How can you forgive these people for killing your family and destroying your life?" Her answer was so sweet and simple. "Forgiveness is all I had to offer," she said. Immaculee discovered God amidst that horrible event.

It was that discovery that allowed her to release herself and her captives from the burden of un-forgiveness. Whenever you think about someone who has lied to you, cheated you, mistreated you or hurt your feelings, just think about Immaculee's story. If she can forgive, surely you can.

"Forgiveness is almost a selfish act because
of its immense benefits to the one who forgives."
~ Lawana Blackwell

Go Ahead and Free Yourself
True forgiveness is when you're able to thank the other person for giving you that particular experience. Without it, you wouldn't be the developed, enlightened person you are today. It really doesn't matter if they deserve the forgiveness or not. You deserve to be released from carrying this burden, and only you can do it.

You are worth it, my friend.

Use No Way as Way

*"We would accomplish many more things
if we did not think of them as impossible."*
~ Vince Lombardi

We live by believing and not by seeing. If you believe that it is impossible to accomplish the big goals you have in your heart without money, right relationships or unlimited resources — you are right. But if you believe that life holds unlimited possibilities for you regardless of your circumstances — then you are also right. We can choose to believe anything, and it then moves from the realm of impossible to possible.

Most people live their lives with the concept that "I will believe it when I see it." This is a person who will never experience the advantages of living an Optimistic Lifestyle and will always experience frustration. You see, signs follow they do not precede. You have to believe first, and then you will "see" it expressed in your life experience.

The Facts Don't Count
God told Abraham, as far as you can "see" that is what I will give to you. Essentially Abraham got to set his own limits. Are far and wide as he was able to believe, he was promised to get it. If he couldn't see past his age, Sarah's age and the deadness of her womb, then he wouldn't get the promises of God. It was all up to the limits he set for himself. Surely when God told Abraham, he would be the father of many nations he might have been inclined to check the facts.

The "facts" that he himself was nearly 100 years old, he had yet to have any children, his wife was also well into her eighties and had clearly passed her childbearing years. It seemed to me, and probably to Abraham and Sarah at the time, to be an impossible situation right there. At this point, after reviewing the facts, Abraham would have had every right to think...yeah right, there is no way that's gonna happen. But instead, Abraham believed God. The facts didn't count.

Zero Limits

I love the philosophy of Bruce Lee. Most know Bruce Lee as an actor, filmmaker, and one of the greatest, most influential martial artists of our time. But one of the things that made Bruce Lee so powerful was his philosophy (mindset).

Bruce Lee is the founder of a system and philosophy of life called Jeet Kune Do. The system works by the use of different "tools" for different situations. It is referred to as a "style without style" or "the art of fighting without fighting," as said by Bruce Lee himself. Jeet Kune Do is not a fixed or patterned martial art form; it is a philosophy. Bruce believed that combat was spontaneous and that a martial artist cannot predict it, only react to it. He felt that a good martial artist should "be like water" and move fluidly without hesitation.

Bruce had many famous quotes, but my favorite is when he said one should "use no way as way" and "have no limitation as limitation." Essentially Bruce was suggesting that we keep an open mind. Don't limit yourself or your thinking. Don't let your beliefs limit your approach to life's experiences.

The Philosophy Behind the Man

Bruce Lee's martial art could not have been as successful and complete without the deep philosophical base he gave it. Martial arts, by nature, are a reflective practice where the practitioner must not only examine the issues of life or death but also the nature of the self. The art of Jeet Kune Do is simply to simplify, and it was one of the paths through which his life revealed its secrets.

The core philosophy of Bruce Lee was to "know you." It is clear that all the avenues Bruce took in life were in pursuit of self-cultivation, which leads to the ultimate destination — self-knowledge. His art and philosophy were the vehicles he used to gain an understanding of

himself, to feel and fully appreciate the experience of what it means to be a human being. To achieve that, he spent countless hours learning, training, reading, and researching.

Bruce's philosophy relates to the truth that the biggest adversary in our life can be ourselves. We are what we are, in a sense, because of the dominating thoughts and beliefs we allow to gather in our head. All concepts of self-improvement, all actions and paths we take, relate solely to our abstract image of ourselves and the world around us. Life is limited only by how we really see ourselves and what we believe about our being. Our effectiveness in life and what we produce is directly related to what we believe is possible.

Cell Phones — The Impossible Becomes Possible

Bruce Lee's philosophy of "use no way as way" is very profound for me. There are so many things that exist today that we once believed were impossible. I remember back in 1984 when I began my first job in corporate working at a mobile communications company, I was fascinated by the fact that this company was selling a breakthrough product called a cellular phone.

As a girl who loved to talk on the phone, I was ecstatic about the thought that now I could talk on the phone while outside the house too. I used to hate to get caught up in the wires while I walked around the room talking to my friends. If I had to run outside to get something or leave the room where the phone base was located, I would have to ask my friends to hold on because I couldn't take the phone with me. Can you imagine? What a dilemma.

As an Assistant Radio Frequency Engineer, it was my responsibility to create coverage predictions and contour maps for the reach of a particular cell site. I then got to drive the map and test the quality of the cellular coverage throughout the test area. I got paid to talk on a phone, in my car (long before that was unacceptable); wow, this was awesome. Something that I thought was previously impossible now was possible. But at that time, the phone was wired through my car and was still limiting me to one physical location.

Certainly this was better than being stuck in my house limited by the length of the phone cord. Now I had a way to communicate with my friends while traveling to and fro. But don't get me wrong… at that time, I was still limited to talking with people within my Cellular Geographical Area or CGA. Otherwise, I would be "roaming." And that was crazy expensive. Plus that phone was so huge, clunky and restrictive and had big large buttons that you could see from space. Still I was the coolest girl in town because I had a mobile phone.

I thought that my mobile phone was the coolest thing ever and surely there was no way it could get better than that. Never would I have dreamed possible that soon after that, someone would have stretched their minds from impossible to possible and create a mobile phone that is nearly the size of a business card and I can talk to my cousin in Trinidad and Tobago or my friend in Dubai from this tiny device that can fit in my pocket.

Were it not for someone willing to use "no way as way," we would not have the Internet, Facebook, Twitter, YouTube or the Smartphone. Probably by the time you read this book, there will be even more inventions and new creations that have come out which reveal how no limitations became the limitation. Maybe you are one of the people who are given a gift that will create something the world can enjoy for generations to come, which we previously thought impossible. You just have to believe that it's possible for you.

The world needs your genius. Just use no way as way.

Honda was Relentless

Most of the important things in this world had been accomplished by people who had kept on trying — even when there seemed to be no hope at all. The story of Soichiro Honda, the founder of the Honda Motor Company, is often told of the most inspirational stories of a man who overcame seemingly insurmountable obstacles on his way to achieving great success. Despite suffering failure, ridicule, and endless financial difficulties, the key to Honda's success was the fact that he used no way as his only way.

Born in 1906 in a small town in Japan known as Komyo, Honda was known to be very creative but a bit of a rebel. (I would suspect

that his give-a-damner was broken at a young age). He spent his early years helping his father with his bicycle repair business. As a young boy, Soichiro had a fascination for machines and how they operated. Later in his life, he had an idea to create a piston ring, a device that moved up and down in a car's engine, which he planned to sell to Toyota. He worked tirelessly, day and night, often sleeping in his workshop, to develop what he believed to be the perfect design.

During the time that he was developing this piston ring, Honda struggled financially. He even had to go so far as to sell his wife's jewelry in order to stay afloat. You can imagine that was not a well-received decision in his household. But Honda kept believing in himself and his vision, in spite of the many obstacles he faced. After completing his piston ring design, Honda went to Toyota as he had planned but was rejected because he was told that his design did not meet the standards of the company. He suffered great ridicule from a lot of people, but this did not stop Honda because he believed both in himself and in the power of his dream. After years of tweaking his product, again through extremely tough economic times, Honda finally perfected his product and won a contract with Toyota.

While it would be nice to end the story there, it doesn't end there. Once Soichiro got the deal with Toyota, he needed to build a factory so that he could fulfill his contractual obligations. At that time, Japan was in war and building supplies were just plain unavailable. Once again, using no way as way, Honda found a way. He developed a concrete making system and, as a result was able to build his factory. But there's more. After his factory was built, it was bombed - not once but twice. Ok, if you're like me at this point I'm thinking, he must have reached his limit. By now, his wife, family, and friends were probably telling him to give it up. Soichiro there is no way you can get this done. He had no money and no factory. Those were the facts. But for Soichiro, no way was the way. The facts didn't count.

Honda rebuilt his factory - again - only to have an earthquake destroy it. Since no limitation was his only limitation, Honda switched gears (pun intended here). He grouped and made lemons out of lemonade. Since there was a gas shortage, Honda had to go back to riding his bicycle.

Using no way as way, Honda ended up creating a small engine for his own bicycle. It became so popular that people wanted it and after much toil, he eventually sold the engine in Japan, Europe, and America. With that small engine, he made the smallest car ever made which eventually grew to became the automotive line we now know as Honda Motor Company.

The rest, of course, is history and now the Honda, the car named after Soichiro Honda, is the car that sells itself.

Believe in your dreams and they will believe in you.

"I am looking for a lot of men
who have an infinite capacity to not know what can't be done."
~ Henry Ford

Coaching for the Impossible
As a Success Coach, I have personally helped hundreds of people step outside of their comfort zones and dare the impossible. What was once their impossible became their reality. There were ways made out of... "Sorry, there just ain't no way."

Many of them are now millionaires as a result of the work we did together. I say together because they were the ones who had to believe what I was telling them was possible for them. Oh sure, they could believe it was possible for me because they saw it. But many did not believe for themselves, yet still they had the courage to rely on me and my faith that they too could live in their dream home or drive their dream car or start the business they always wanted to start, in spite of the facts in front of them.

Those people who held my hands so tightly as I helped escort them into success are my heroes. They wanted more from their lives but were afraid to believe the impossible alone, so I helped. I always tell my clients that a good coach sings your life's song back to you when you forget the words. So, I kept singing and they kept believing.

122

Love Extravagantly

"Love is the magician
that pulls man out of his own hat."
~ Ben Hecht

Getting through this journey successfully absolutely requires that you make it a regular habit to walk in love. This is the first and greatest commandment. But before we get into exactly how and why we must walk in love. We must first examine the concept of love. Right off the bat, let me tell you that Love is not a feeling. Love is a person. It is written that whoever does not love, knows not God because God is Love. (1 John 4:7-8)

> If you want to get an insight into the nature (or personality of God simply study what love is. It is written (see 1 Corinthians 13) that;
> Love is patient and kind.
> Love is not jealous or boastful or proud or rude.
> Love does not demand its own way.
> Love is not irritable, and it keeps no record of when it has been wronged.
> Love is never glad about injustice but rejoices whenever the truth wins out.
> Love never gives up, never loses faith, is always hopeful, and endures through every circumstance.

That my friends is God since God is love. When we walk in love, we are walking in the form of God. There is no greater feeling than that.

Commanded to Love

So, when above all else, we have been commanded to love, we are in

123

essence being commanded to be God. Love is not an option. We have not been commanded to like; that would take away your free will. We don't have to like everyone or everything. We were however commanded to love. There are millions of songs about it, and movies about it and even holidays celebrating it but do we really understand love. I cannot love you only when you do right by me, I must love you because it is my responsibility to love you.

Besides, our Faith is powered by love. So, if you don't have love, your Faith won't work. Period.

Plainly speaking, Love is the curtain rod upon which everything else discussed in this book hangs. If you are not walking in love, your journey will be very tumultuous and contentious. If you are seeking peace, you must walk in love. The more deeply you love, the deeper you will experience a joy that few will ever know.

"I have found the paradox that if you love until it hurts, there can be no more hurt, only more love.
- Mother Teresa

Whenever I'm feeling out of sorts or find myself in an adversarial situation with someone, which is now not very often, I make it a habit to apply love to the situation. I have been hurt by people who have done what some may consider unforgivable things, but I had to look at the situation, and that person, through the eyes of love if I wanted to get past it. Not for them but for me.

Once I did that, I took my power back, the one the ego lied and told me I lost, and then it was very difficult to see the situation the same way any longer. I used to think that you had to fight for what you wanted or for what was right in the world. I now know that you must fight nothing, absolutely nothing. Instead, agree with everything and everyone. Love extravagantly.

Loving Extravagantly — The Greatest Secret
To do something extravagantly is to exceed reasonable bounds. To go all out, above and beyond. That is how God loves you..and me. While we

may not love the actions of people, we must never withhold our love from them. But don't fall into the misconception that you fall into love. Love is a decision. I would argue that love is not even an emotion. It's not even about feelings. We cannot trust those. Feelings and emotions change all the time. I'm talking about love as an action. A state of being. An approach.

Love is sort of like the engine that makes everything else work. Without love, nothing else really matters. Of all of the other life-changing secrets I share with you here in this book, learning how to love extravagantly is the greatest of all secrets. It just shouldn't be a secret anymore.

Ever Expanding Love

Don't worry if you think you've used up all of your love. You'll never run out of love. There's more where that came from. I remember when my babies were born, I felt a love that was unlike anything that I have ever felt before. It carried with it no conditions and no limits. It is pure.

When Evan was born on 6/14/1988, I thought that it was impossible to love another person the way I loved him. It was a love that was so strong and powerful; it was impossible to put into words. I thought it would be unfair to have another child because surely I had given all my love to this child. I didn't think I could find any more. It took nine years to the day for me to realize that I had more love to give. On 6/14/1997 Taylor was born and miraculously I found more love, that same kind of unspeakable love I had for Evan. After that, I thought surely I have used up all of my love, but as fate would have it on 8/25/1998 at 6:14 pm once again my love tank found expansion when Myles was born. I never knew a love like this one before.

Each time one of them walks in a room, I'm convinced that angels are singing. Maybe it's just me but I think my babies are perfect. One day, late at night, when they were all sleeping, I went into each of the boys' rooms and I just stared at them wondering if God could possibly love me more than I love these guys I was the luckiest girl alive.

Advice from Cousin Tillie
When I was a young wife, some of the best advice that I received was from my cousin, Tillie. She and her husband Mickey as far as I was concerned, other than my parents, had the model relationship. They were so loving and affectionate to each other, always smooching and speaking to each other in loving ways. As I was a little girl, I remember thinking, "When I get married, I want to have a marriage like that." So when I was about to marry, I inquired of Tillie about what the secret was to a great marriage.

Of course, there were many things she told me. But the main thing she said was to learn to bite your tongue. She told me that men didn't like nagging wives, wives who murmur or complain. She told me that you often have to make a decision to be married or a decision to be right, and sometimes, often, you cannot be both. I learned that through applying loving language, even at times of disagreement, and managing your tongue, you can actually win them over through that love.

> "Your mate doesn't live by bread alone; he or she needs to be "buttered up" from time to time."
> - Zig Ziglar

The Love Factor
Let love be the deciding factor you multiply to every situation and circumstance. Be kinder than necessary. Look at the situation through loving lenses. Don't worry that you feel the other person mistakes your kindness for weakness. It actually takes strength to love. You will never lose with love. Love always wins.

Let the people you love know it all the time. Because I applied this strategy, I Love You were the last three words I said to my mother and her to me before she transitioned.

If you don't believe me on this love thing, you're going to have to trust me on this one. Paul told the Corinthians, and I tell you:

We don't yet see things clearly. We're squinting in a fog, peering through a mist. But it won't be long before the weather clears, and the sun shines bright. We'll see it all then, see it all as clearly as God sees us, knowing him directly just as he knows us. But for right now, until that completeness, we have three things to do to lead us toward that consummation: Trust steadily in God, hope unswervingly, love extravagantly. And the best of the three is love. - 1 Corinthians 13:12-13

The truth is; Love is Divine. God Himself is Love. Whoever lives in love lives in God and God in them.

Do not withhold your love under any circumstances. Love your enemies, love your haters, and love those you believe to be unlovable. It is amazing what love can do. It has miracle-working power.

Every time you love, the Universe shifts.

PART FOUR

RELATIONSHIP
WITH
SPIRIT

You Must Be Born Again,
and Again, and Again

"My soul is from elsewhere, I'm sure of that,
and I intend to end up there."
~ Rumi

Countless times, I'd think to myself, If God would just take this cup from me, I'd be better off. The cup symbolizes an unpleasant situation and or circumstance. I often wonder if Jesus felt the same way at the cross. If he knew there was something he needed to do, but even he would have preferred getting it done another way. Those were my sentiments at those times in my life.

So many times along the journey, the pain and fear have been so great I have often wished for another way, an alternative. But most times, there was no other way to get around the storm except to grow right, straight through it. Sometimes you just have to P.U.S.H. (Pray Until Shift Happens)

Birthing Our Blessings

The process of giving birth is similar. As you get closer and closer to actually giving birth to your blessing — a higher expression of yourself — the contractions, aka pain, become more intense and more frequent. While I may have given birth to three beautiful sons, I have also given birth to myself, over and over again.

At each point, when I was just about to have a breakthrough in some area of my life, the contractions would become more intense and frequent. In these instances, the contractions came in the form of conflict, fear and/or worry. But I kept breathing, as in the Lamaze technique. I pushed a little, breathed a little, and got through the delivery, only to find the most beautiful blessing on the other side of the pain.

They say that after you give birth, you forget the pain once you hold your bundle of joy. I'm not entirely sure that I can confirm that as true, however, what I can say is it's worth it in the end.

I've learned over the years that we are all on a constant journey of growth and development until we surrender this body and turn it in for a new model. Often you can go through years of mundane quietness and then all of a sudden it rains. And as the saying goes, when it rains it pours. Maybe you lost your job, and then your car breaks down, your child's tuition is past-due, and your wife/husband has decided to go back to school and quit his/her job. Then, if that's not enough, one of your parents gets ill and requires your full-time care and attention.

Guess what, my friend, you're in labor.

"Be the kind of person that when your feet hit the floor in the morning the devil says "Damn, s/he's up"
- Unknown Author

You Can Do This... Just Push!
I've been in an actual delivery/labor room three different times throughout my life. Each of those times, I can remember thinking, If I could just get up out of this bed, tell all these people to leave this hospital room because I've changed my mind, I would. If I could have just yelled out and let them all know that I had decided not to go through with it, I would have. But I couldn't. Getting out of that "labor" was not an option, so I had to go through with it. There was no way out of that room, except to accomplish that delivery.

For some reason, all three of my deliveries had to be induced with the assistance of a synthetic oxytocin. A laboring woman normally produces natural oxytocin, but it is sometimes necessary to augment or speed up the labor process with the use of a synthetic oxytocin. Synthetically induced contractions will often be more forceful, last much longer, and come closer together. So, if the normal process of delivery was not challenging enough, imagine intensifying it with an amplifier that simply turns the dial up several notches, increasing the pain's intensity, speed, and longevity.

132

As someone who was, and still is, always searching for deeper meaning, I needed to make sense of the birth process. Since I knew that there is always a corresponding spiritual event to every natural event, I was in search of the spiritual significance of giving birth.

I remember when I was in labor with my first son, I was young and had no idea how the process worked. He was in an occipito-posterior position, which is a fancy way of saying the back of his head was down, and he was facing up — towards heaven perhaps. This meant that the back of his skull was pressing against the back of my pelvis. While most babies are born with their heads facing down, he was born looking up. These types of births are more difficult and painful. The pain is more concentrated in the mother's back region. Due to the position of the baby's head, it makes pushing almost impossible, but not entirely impossible. Although the baby may at some point be in that posterior position, it is very rare for the baby to remain in that position through to birth — but not for my babies.

Two of my sons, the first son, and second son were both born "face up" from that posterior position. Perhaps it had something to do with being born to the Queen of Optimism, but the fact that my first two babies were born looking up is pretty remarkable. The doctor told me at the time that this only happens in one in every 3,500 births.

To make it even rarer, both boys were born on the exact same day — nine years apart! The pain of their births was intense due to their positioning, and even more intensified with the help of the synthetic oxytocin. Here I was a young girl without a clue and without a choice. I had to go — or grow — through that experience. At one point, the nurse, when I asked her what we could do to relieve the pain, told me, "There is nothing you can do. That's why they call it labor, honey." Let's just say I didn't like her very much at that moment.

But this was the same nurse who refused to let them give me a cesarean when the doctor had run out of patience and thought I was unable to deliver the baby on my own. That seemingly mean nurse whispered in my ear, as they had already called the anesthesiologist and prepped me for surgery, and she told me, "Sweetheart, you can do this. Just get mad enough to push this baby out." With the encouragement of that midwife, I did just that.

Since then, I have made it my life's work to serve as a "midwife" for others. I have witnessed people giving birth to their own miracles, be it a career change, buying and saving their dream home, starting a new business, or finding and marrying the love of their life. I've held their hand, rubbed their backs, prayed with them, and even cried with them. But all the while, I've been there whispering in their ear. And when it looked like it couldn't get done, I said, "Sweetheart, you can do this... just push."

And Keep on Pushing

I was born again the same day Evan was born, and then again with Taylor, and then again with Myles, and then again each time I graduated to renewing my own mind. Sometimes I feel like I am born again every morning because it is another chance to grow.

I love the artists who are constantly reinventing themselves. Madonna, Cher, Beyonce. Hey, maybe it's the single name that does the trick. Anyway, I am amazed how they continue to stay relevant in changing times.

When my friend Teri took me to see Cher recently, I was in awe of this 68-year-old woman who could still sell out a stadium full of admirers. Cher evolved and yet she remained true to herself. That's really the secret. Evolving but remaining. It's a careful balance. Cher wore the same outfits she had on 35 years ago, but with the appropriate modifications for a woman of her "seasoning." Her voice was still fresh, her look was contemporary, and her show was spectacular.

Cher inspired me that night. She lifted me to a new place. It was that night that I decided if this woman who is 20 years my senior could keep pushing, then I could keep pushing. I could keep evolving because there is much more to do. Once more, I was born again.

Your Arms Are Too Short
to Box with God

"When you are going through things and wonder where God is, remember this...The teacher is always quiet during a test."
~ Unknown

I've got news for you... God is not mad at you. Let's get that straight right off the top.

Trust in God

I've been asked to speak on this topic many times. At one point, I was part of a panel that included a minister, a psychologist, a mental health professional and even a former nun. The entire discussion centered on a group of people I would certainly include in the category of Frustrated Believers. These people at one time or another had a relationship with God. However, somewhere along the way, they found themselves mad at God and truly believed God was mad at them too. They attended church but were disillusioned and disappointed. Usually not by God but by God's "people". Frankly they were all "churched out." They were tired of empty, repetitive sermons and preaching from people whose lives did not show evidence of what they were espousing.

They believed in God, even prayed, but were frustrated by a lack of understanding why they did not see results. Somehow, they felt they were not "doing" enough or were not being "good" enough to please what they saw as a difficult, judgmental God. I was brought on the panel to bring a perspective as the Queen of Optimism on how to stay optimistic when it seems like God is on vacation.

The discussion became quite emotional at times. People couldn't understand why God would sit around permitting the injustice, poverty and suffering to continue in our world. When I tried to offer some intelligent and profound answers, all I could think of to share were the words Paul wrote to the Romans when he said, "Think rightly about yourself and God."

What Paul is saying essentially and still to this day I find to be true is that people reduce God down to human standards and characteristics. We expect God to act like we would in a similar situation, and this is just not the case. Firstly, God's ways are not our ways. God forbid. You see, it is written that God is not human, that he should lie, not a human being, that he should change his mind. Our unfaithfulness will never frustrate God's faithfulness. The certainty of all God's promises rests on His character, not on our faithfulness. Thank God for that.

"Our idea of God tells us more about ourselves than about Him."
~ Thomas Merton

You Are the Answer & Solution

In my research, I've found two main things that displease God. First, it is clearly written that without Faith, it is impossible to please Him. The other thing God called evil was when he saw kings, princes and queens walking around like slaves, meaning that it displeases God to see us living below our privilege. When we permit things to go on and accept things that are not excellent and the best, God calls that evil.

Meanwhile, we must stop looking outside of ourselves to solve the answers of this world. To the questions of your life, you are the answer. To the problems of your life, you are the solution. When you realize that there is nothing lacking, the whole world belongs to you.

How Do You See God?

You see, we see God as we see ourselves. If you're unforgiving, you see God that way. If you're judgmental of others, you see God as judgmental of you. If you're loving, kind and forgiving, you'll see God that same way. It's not what God sees in you; it's what you see in you that matters most. You were created in God's image, not the other way around. Frankly, the concept of God needs to be re-presented.

The Bible's purpose and message has been misconstrued and requires a new set of eyes. The Bible is not some book that tells you all that "thou shalt not do." The Bible is a GPS (Global Positioning System) of sorts. It's a self-help guide whose purpose is to lift you higher, not tear you down. It is designed to encourage, not discourage. To bring good news, not doom and gloom. It shows what you're liberated to do, instead of what you're restricted from doing.

This is why I believe so strongly in living an optimistic lifestyle. It is only by changing the way you look at things that those things change. One day I realized that I was not a human being having a spiritual experience, but instead I was a spiritual being having a human experience. That's when things began to clear up for me.

We Are Here to Work on Ourselves

For some reason, popular belief is that this life is not about you. This is wrong; it's all about you. You are the center of it all. It's been you all the time. There's no greater work that any of us is responsible for doing except to work on ourselves. We are not to try to change people or to try and change things. We are only responsible for changing ourselves. This begins with changing how you see yourself. Stop fighting with God. For you to get action from God, you are going to have to agree with God. Stop battling with a God, who thinks you are worth dying for. You're simply fighting with yourself after all. Besides that is not a fight you will win. Your arms are too short to box with God.

Is it not written in the Bible (Psalm 82:6, John 10:34) that "I said you are 'gods.'"?

This requires more study and discussion than I can cover in this chapter. But I urge you to start asking some important questions. Start challenging what you were taught and begin to think for yourself. I am inquisitive; I've always been that way. If things didn't make sense to me, I sought for answers. That is one of the keys to getting through this journey successfully. We are all on a treasure hunt trying to find the City of Gold. Maybe it's time we realize, we are already there.

Buy Your Religion Wholesale

"To find yourself, think for yourself."
~ Socrates

I grew up in church. It's funny when I think back on the Shelley Roxanne at five years old, whose only job on Easter Sunday was to deliver three short words — Happy Easter Day — to the small congregation at Calvary Baptist Church. Still, it just wasn't happening. Five-year-old Shelley Roxanne just stood there next to Cousin George and others but couldn't/wouldn't deliver her lines. I was terrified. I grabbed my dad's leg and hid behind him where everything was safe — and still is — and cried the ugly cry. You know that kind of cry that makes even a cute face look ugly.

Still, I hardly ever missed a Sunday at church throughout most of my young life. I was on a search for truth and authenticity. But I quickly realized that being in church no more made you a Christian than being in a garage made you a car.

Being baptized at nine years old surely sealed the deal for me. I was in like Flynn — or at least I thought so. I had no idea who God was, so surely I had no idea who I was in Him. I attended Sunday School, was on the Junior Usher Board, and sang in the Children's Choir. Still I hadn't met God personally.

"I like your Christ; I do not like your Christians.
Your Christians are so unlike your Christ."
~ Mahatma Gandhi

139

Looking for My God

As I grew, I left that home church and joined a different church in search for more understanding. While God had likely made appearances in this church, he was definitely not a regular. All that I had learned there about God — and me — came second-hand from people who claimed to know Him far better than I did.

But something was amiss. Many of the church folks could quote scripture as if they were rap lyrics. But their lives did not show evidence consistent with what they were quoting. Even so, I still wanted to know the God that they spoke of. The one who sacrificed his son for me, the one who made provisions for me to live an abundant life — that God. Not the one they were showing me, the one I had to wait on, to beg, the one who was temperamental, judgmental and mean.

> *"To believe in something, and not to live it, is dishonest."*
> ~ Mahatma Gandhi

Going Directly to the Source

Once I finally met the God of the Bible directly, I was hooked. You mean, I don't have to be broke if I don't want to be? You mean, I don't have to be sick, or in fear, or poor in order to prove my sacrifice, my worthiness? Surely money is the root of all evil, at least that's how the "church folks" made it seem. That was only until I learned it was because they didn't have any. Or did they not have any because of what they believed about money?

Well, I wanted that abundant life but was that in store for me? Oh, it is? Cool, then this is the God I've been looking for. But I had to find Him on my own. Not get Him second-hand from people whose lives were inconsistent with his Word. I had to buy my religion wholesale and go directly to the manufacturer, instead of through middlemen as I had early on.

While you should buy your religion wholesale, when you eventually find the pearl (that thing of great value which you're seeking), you must pay all you've got to buy it. This is likened to what Matthew wrote about when he referred to the merchant seeking beautiful pearls who, when

140

he had found one pearl of great price, went and sold all that he had and bought it. (See Matthew 13:45-46.)

Once again this is a metaphor written here in Matthew. He is not talking about you spending all your money or selling everything you have, the meaning here is much deeper. Matthew suggests here that when we find that thing that makes us come alive, that truth that is more valuable than anything else, we should give up all the other limiting thoughts and beliefs we now possess and do whatever we have to do to own the treasure of our own truth.

Find Your Treasure —Your God

Be sure not to let anyone turn you off from finding what makes you come alive. Just because you may be turned off by the representations — or misrepresentations — of what others have demonstrated regarding what a spiritual life looks like, don't let anyone cause you not to get to know your God (and yourself). It's worth everything you've got to find such a treasure.

Come Out of the Closet

"He who trims himself to suit everyone
will soon whittle himself away."
~ Raymond Hull

When I began hosting The Shelley Roxanne Show on the radio, one of the first things they told me was that I could discuss just about anything I wanted with few exceptions. The only exceptions were politics and religion. It's common for celebrities and or public figures to refrain from conversations about these two topics, especially discussing their faith. Common dogma is not to mix church and state.

Even so, those were two of the first topics I discussed on my show. And on a regular basis, they were weaved into the Hot Topics that we spoke about on the program. I recognize that the subject of religion is controversial, but I must use my platform to give people the permission to talk about it. It's important.

Now, having lived in both the North part of the USA for most of my journey and then in the South in recent years, I found a major distinct difference between people's comfort level in expressing their faith and beliefs in public. In the South, I found that people did not hide their faith in public as much as they did in the North. I was impressed to find that while Bibles were taken out of the schools nationwide, the sports teams, in both public and private schools, still openly prayed before, and after, sporting events — especially football games. Maybe this is why God loves football, at least that's from a Football Mom's perspective!

Exploring Stereotypes
I was always moved by the courage of my Jewish friends who had the

chutzpah to wear their yamakas (Jewish headgear, also known as kippahs) in public, especially in the corporate arena. I say it was courageous because they subjected themselves to possibly being judged by others.

When I was doing diversity training in the corporate world, we did a fascinating exercise on stereotypes. We put up large poster-size paper all over the room. On each piece of poster paper, we wrote the name of a particular group of people —e.g. Blacks, Whites, Jewish, Asian, Hispanic, Gays, etc. We covered a wide array of groups related to gender, race, sexual orientation and the like. We then provided the participants with markers and instructed them to go around the room and write under the heading any stereotypes that they heard and/or believed about that particular group.

Of course, we had to make it a "safe room," by assuring each participant to feel safe that they would not be judged for what they wrote down. I was always amazed at how long it took the participants to feel comfortable with writing down known stereotypes about racial groups. But they were quick to write down the stereotypes for religious groups and groups related to sexual orientation.

A stereotype by its own definition is an oversimplified image or idea about a particular group of people. It was surprising to find in the hundreds and hundreds of sessions I conducted that the very same stereotypes kept coming up over and over again about particular groups. Over the years, we have watched stereotypes change. But the only way they are changed is when people who are members of those groups come out and dispel those stereotypes by how they live their lives in public.

Living Publicly Dispels Stereotypes
I once did a show I called "Are Gays the New Black?" With the help of the awesome Louis Thorpe, an openly gay man, I was able to explore so many stereotypes about gay men. Louis is a tall, athletic man whose personal appearance certainly does not fit the typical stereotype of gay. That's why I was so excited to interview him. Louis subjected himself to the silly questions that I asked him in order to refute much of what people falsely believed about gay people. That was an awesome show.

This show was done back in 2007 when the world was not even

as open as it is right now about this subject. But Louis said something that really stayed with me. He told me that if you put 25 gay people in a room, you would have 25 different opinions about most areas of life — including what it means to be gay.

Most of us could probably say the very same thing about any group we are a part of. If you don't like how your group(s) are being stereotyped in the world, come out of the closet and dispel it. You don't have to stand on your soap box or come on my radio show to do it — just do you. Live free of fear of what other people think of you.

It took a major celebrity like Ellen DeGeneres to "come out" in order to give other gays and lesbians — celebrities and otherwise — permission to do the same. There are wonderful stories of people who got the courage to come out to their family and friends after Ellen came out publicly. Ellen was free, and those people wanted to be free as well.

"Let the redeemed of the Lord say so."
~ Psalm 107:2

Why Be a Closet Believer?

Most people who have a problem with someone expressing their true self to the world is likely someone who is living in the closet in some way or another themselves. Far too many of the people I have coached were experiencing so much frustration in their lives because they were in hiding in the closet about their faith/beliefs. While they went to church or temple, they somehow contained that belief into the four walls of that church, synagogue, temple, etc.

So for two hours on Saturday or Sunday, they went to their place of worship. Perhaps they read a scripture, sang a song or two, and then left the building, and all the power that came with it stayed inside. Why be a closet Christian, Catholic, Jew or Muslim? If you have the courage to believe in a God you do not see, surely you should have the courage to be open about it. That's pretty bold after all to have that belief in the first place.

It's written that blessed are those who do not see and yet believe. Actually for most followers of Jesus, it is a requirement to be out of the closet. In many parts of the scripture, Jesus said, "Everyone who acknowledges me publicly here on earth, the Son of Man will also acknowledge in the presence of God's angels."

But I get it, it's just not popular. It never has been. But I am suggesting that if you want to live a maximized life — free of fear, shame, frustration and guilt — you must live free.

It's time to come out of the closet. Everyone else is, so why not you — the Believer.

Got Faith?

*"Sometimes your only available transportation
is a leap of faith."*
~ Margaret Shepard

I'm going to get quite frank here. If you don't have Faith, you will not achieve the things you want in your life. It's just that simple. Faith is the primary factor in whether or not you will experience a full life. Without it, you cannot please God (or yourself). Faith is so important that instead of trying to get more money you should try to get more Faith. Faith is the universal currency. You can acquire anything with Faith.

Faith is to your life what an engine is to a car. You can have a beautiful sports car, your dream car; it can have the most incredible wheels/rims you have ever seen. It can have a transmission, a steering system, brakes, tires, etc. However, without an engine, that car will not work. The same goes for your life without Faith in it.

The best way that I have found to treat Faith is like a person. I like to think of Faith as my best personal assistant. If I need something done in my life — no matter how major — I can give it to Faith, and she will take care of it.

Faith's attributes:
Faith has unlimited skills.
Faith works without breaks.
Faith has unlimited capacity.
There is nowhere Faith can't or won't go.
There is nothing that Faith can't or won't do.
Faith drives you anywhere you want to go.

Faith works for you 24/7/365.
Faith takes no vacations or sick days.
Faith works exclusively for you.
You don't need to check up on Faith because you can be
confident she is doing what she is instructed to do.
Faith can work miracles.
Faith makes the impossible possible. Nothing is impossible
for Faith.
Faith works fast.
You can meet and exceed all of your goals using Faith.

How to use Faith:
Faith must regularly be fed.
Faith only follows your words (Be careful how you instruct
Faith; she is rather literal.)
Faith does not know when you're joking.
Faith does not judge and is never insubordinate.
The more you work Faith, the better she performs.
Don't let Faith go idle; keep her working.
Trust Faith; believe in Faith's power.
Fear is Faith's kryptonite; keep it away from her.
Faith will not work when Fear is present. Fear undermines
Faith.
Faith has unlimited potential, but a demand must be
placed on her.

Without Faith, life can seem to be a meaningless series of
ups and downs. Yet…
Faith can find you the man (or woman) of your dreams.
Faith can get you a job.
Faith can heal.
Faith can get you a brand-new house.
Faith can restore your broken marriage.

I highly recommend Faith and would give her a strong recommendation. If Faith is not working, she is unemployed. Paul wrote in his letter to James that "Faith by itself if it does not have works is dead."

It is written that "According to your faith, be it unto you." This adage sums up exactly the life that we have and the results we get in every situation. If your Faith is weak, your results will be weak. If your Faith is strong, and you keep your Faith deployed, your results will be powerful as well.

In fact, your Faith has to exercised, like a muscle. If not, you will lose your Faith dexterity.

Jeff is a gym rat. He loves to go to the gym (a love we do not share). He told me that when he has not been to the gym for a while, and he attempts to go back, it is impossible for him to lift the amount of weight he was used to lifting. Isn't that the same with Faith? Don't let your faith sit down, always keep Faith working. Keep your Faith's dexterity.

Looking Closer at Faith
Faith is belief without sense evidence. Faith is a firm conviction in something for which there may be no tangible proof. Faith is not a feeling; Faith is confidence in God. Faith means being sure of the things we hope for and knowing that something is real, even if we do not see it. Faith is a gift that you have been given by God. Faith is like money; the more you have, the more you can do.

Without Faith, you cannot win. On the other hand, nothing can withstand Faith. Faith is the most valuable asset you'll ever possess.

The just shall live by Faith.

"This is the confidence we have in approaching God:
that if we ask anything according to His will, He hears us.
And if we know that he hears us—whatever we ask—
we know that we have what we asked of him."
~ 1 John 5:14-15

Whatever you have to do, you must contend for Faith. You must fight for Faith. The Bible tells us that the only fight we are to engage in is "the good fight of faith." (See 1 Tim 6:12.)

The foundation of optimism is all about Faith. The concept of the glass half-empty versus the glass half-full is all about Faith. The pessimist looks only at what it can see with the naked eye. The pessimist looks at what is in the glass and sees limits and lack. Meanwhile, the optimist focuses on what is not seen with the naked eye. The optimist looks at the glass through the eyes of Faith and sees unlimited possibilities.

Biblical Stories of Faith

There are numerous accounts in the Bible exemplifying demonstrations of how someone's Faith caused them to experience great, miraculous things. There was the woman who had been bleeding for 12 years and could not find a cure, although she had spent all of her money on doctors. However, she had repeatedly stated that if she were just to touch Jesus' clothing that she would be made whole (healed and restored).

This woman acted on her Faith, and she was eventually able to press her way through the crowd to where Jesus stood. When she took action on her belief, the bleeding immediately stopped, and the woman was healed. When Jesus realized what had happened to the woman, he told her, "Daughter, your faith has healed you." (See Luke 8:48, Mark 5:34, and Matthew 9:22.) Notice that Jesus did not take credit for her healing; he gave the credit to her Faith.

The same is true for a woman whose daughter was ill, and she asked Jesus for mercy. When he challenged her about whether she was entitled to it, she was unrelenting in her belief that she was entitled. (She had that knowing). As a result, he told her, "Woman, you have strong faith therefore what you wanted will be done for you." At that very moment, her daughter was cured. Again, it was not what he did or did not do, it was her Faith that cured her daughter. (Matthew 15:28)

As we discussed previously, this Faith thing works for anyone. The best example of that was the matter of the Centurion man of Capernaum. This man was a Roman Captain, who approached Jesus and told him that his servant was very ill and in a lot of pain. Jesus immediately offered to

go to the Captain's servant, who was about 20 miles away, and heal him.

But the Roman Captain said, "Oh no, I don't want to put you through all of that trouble. You don't need to come to my house; just speak the word from right here where you are, and I believe my servant will be fine."

Jesus was astounded by this man's Faith. Jesus directed the Roman officer to go on his way, and his servant would be healed just as he believed. And sure enough, the servant was healed at that very moment. Jesus turned to the crowd following him and told them that he had not seen such a great demonstration of Faith, even amongst the people who are supposed to know God and how he works. (Matthew 8:5-13)

Faith Is Your Servant
Faith works not just for healing, but for every other area of life which permits you to accomplish worthwhile goals. Faith is your servant; put Faith to work for you.

Guard Your Heart

"Above all else, guard your heart with all diligence,
for it determines the course of your life."
~ Proverbs 4:23

The message in the above proverb clearly is not just a passing suggestion. It sounds pretty important to me. It is written "above all else," which clearly signifies that the heart — your heart — is something to be treasured. Above all else suggests that while there are other things you must do, guarding your heart is of the utmost importance. When I refer to the heart, I'm not speaking of the physical heart pump, but of the spiritual reference to the heart.

How Things Are Stored
Our hearts are the home for our mainframe computer. The programming of that computer determines how we see the world. You see, we have two minds — the conscious mind and the subconscious mind. The subconscious mind is powerful. It's actually like a super computer with the ability to process millions of bits of information at one given time. Your subconscious mind is also the seat of your emotions, imagination, long-term memory, and all of your behavior patterns.

The programming that takes place in the subconscious mind, the super processor — located in the heart — filters everything and sends it to the conscious mind for action. The conscious mind, on the other hand, can only process a few bits of information at one time — but this is where the analytics take place. The conscious mind takes in the info, and the subconscious mind processes it for storage and later use. This process takes place very quickly and without your knowledge and or permission

— at least not the conscious mind's knowledge.

This is why it's critical to be careful what you allow into the subconscious mind. It is your hard drive, and just like any other computer, you must have a firewall and anti-virus software to protect it from damage. Keep in mind, your subconscious mind does not critique or analyze anything. It simply responds directly to its program. It does not know right from wrong or fantasy from reality. It only responds to its programming.

A good man brings good things out of the good stored up in the treasury of his heart, and an evil man brings evil things out of the evil stored up in the treasury of his heart. A treasury is a place where valuable things are stored. How someone really feels and/or believes about particular things, people, etc. is stored or hidden in the treasury of their heart.

Ultimately what you say, or speak, how you behave, how you process information and how you perceive situations all come directly from what's stored in the treasury. This is why it's so important to guard or protect what goes into the treasury, because from it flows the springs of life.

Beware of What You Take In

For those of you who need a more practical quote, let me give you this one: You are what you eat. I don't mean "eat" in the actual sense of consuming food, I mean the food you feed your heart and mind… the information you take in on a daily basis… what and who you expose yourself to in your life. Do I suggest you live in a monastery up in the mountains and talk to no one? Of course not. However, I do suggest you be more careful of what you consume or take in or become conscious (knowledgeable) of. Nothing, and I mean nothing, is real or can affect you, except the consciousness you have of it. Said another way, what you don't know won't hurt you. The same applies here.

As we see in the "self-help book" in Genesis, Chapter 3, God did not want Adam and Eve to experience evil. So he didn't want them to take consciousness of evil by eating the fruit of the Tree of the Knowledge of Good and Evil. Because when you take consciousness or knowledge of

something not good for you, by consumption you pay a dear price. What we are conscious of is the only cause of what we experience in life. There can be no change unless and until we change what we are conscious of. You must guard your heart.

You must protect your heart like you would protect a little child. I remember when my son, Evan, was a baby. We used to call him "the boy in the plastic bubble." When our children are infants, we sterilize everything that goes into their mouths and we insist that anyone who touches the newborn bundle of joy must wash their hands — well at least we do this with the first child. For every subsequent child, we seem to ease up on the rules. Nonetheless, we protect our infants because they are precious, tender and delicate. They cannot protect themselves and are dependent upon us as parents to do it for them.

When you first begin the process of guarding your heart, it may start out just like that. You may be overly cautious in the beginning. However, once you build up your heart's immune system, it will begin to protect itself automatically.

The Impact of Our Hearts
The only way to change a man's actions and his thinking is by changing the condition of his heart. What a man holds in his heart, or thinks have a great effect on every aspect of his life experience. He is affected not just mentally, but also spiritually, physically and financially.

For instance, poverty is not a condition of the pocketbook — it is a condition of the heart. A man is poor because he thinks he is or is conscious of being poor. Whereas a rich man is rich because he thinks he is rich. The same if he thinks he is sick; he must experience sickness. For this reason, you must be especially concerned with the condition of your heart.

We view the world through our hearts. Actually what we see with our eyes and hear with our ears is colored by the condition of our hearts. It's where everything is processed before reaction. Our heart determines our response to the issues of our lives.

Being Mindful of Our Hearts

The only way to change what you're experiencing in life is to change your heart. Twenty-four hours a day, seven days a week, your heart is being programmed with information and data. It's the most sophisticated of computers because the programming goes in without you having to physically put it in there. You can actually be in the wrong place at the wrong time hearing the wrong thing, and suddenly you have been programmed.

To guard your heart includes being mindful of the books you read, the movies you watch, the music you listen to, and the people you hang out with. The concept is garbage in, garbage out. We tell this to our teenagers as they grow up, but we don't realize that it's as important for us to do the same as adults as well.

Our heart is the truest expression of who we really are. It is delicate and can be broken. Many people have died from a broken heart. Now we all know that a broken heart is not a literal term — or is it? When your heart is broken, the beliefs that you held there have been shattered or destroyed by the acquisition of new information. Again, your heart is a safe haven for special things and should be protected with all your might.

Have you ever received a package from FedEx or UPS? The delivery person requires you to sign for the package so you can acknowledge to the sender your receipt of the package. There have been times when a delivery person attempted to deliver a package to me but after inspection it was determined that the package did not belong to me. I refused it and would not sign for it. When you sign for it, you endorse it — acknowledging your acceptance of that package. You must do the same thing when people try and put things — i.e. negative attributes — on you that you don't want and or deserve. If someone calls you incompetent or stupid, simply do not sign for that package. It is not yours and you don't have to accept it into your treasury.

You must protect yourself from the things that will rob you of your optimistic outlook. Do you ever wonder why and how unwelcome thoughts come into your mind often out of the blue? They come from the "other" mind or the subconscious mind's previous exposure. It's like catching a cold. Somewhere, somehow you were exposed to someone with a "cold" and you caught it. The cold came upon you without your permission but with your allowance. You must also protect your heart from viruses and contamination.

Whether it is certain television shows, news reports, movies or even people, the overwhelming influences of daily life threaten to decay even the most tender of hearts. Guard yours with all diligence because the source of your life flows from it.

PART FIVE

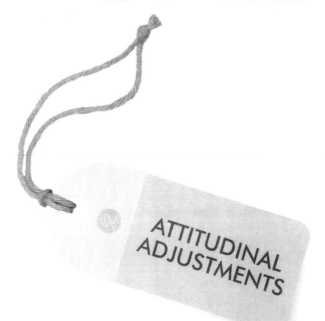

ATTITUDINAL
ADJUSTMENTS

Go on the Negaholic's Diet®

*"An attitude of positive expectation is
the mark of the superior personality."*
~ Brian Tracy

A few years ago, I announced on the radio that I do not read the newspaper or watch the news on television. You wouldn't believe the flack that I got from some people who were just downright appalled by the fact that I didn't glue myself to the paper and the TV getting the latest news. My feeling is that there is no "good news" in the paper or on television.

It's not helpful to me or my optimistic outlook to know that someone was murdered last night or maimed in a terrible accident or that the President raised the terror alert to every color in the rainbow. That kind of food that people eat upon every day must affect them adversely. I won't eat it. Believe me, if there were information that you needed to have, like some emergency that requires you to take immediate action, someone would let you know. Otherwise, you should think on good things because you are what you eat.

Each time someone wants to tell me something, I feel like breaking out in song like the lady in The Wiz who proclaims "don't nobody bring me no bad news." The same people I knew who felt that my diet of "no bad news" was irresponsible found themselves depressed and sad on a regular basis. However, over time and by listening to Optimistic Radio, they had a change of heart. They were provided with new information that proved perhaps that they should modify their daily diets to a more healthy input of positive, good "food."

Negativity's Bad Effects
If you don't think that negative information has a direct effect on you physically than let's take a moment to examine lie detectors — also known as polygraphs. I believe we are all wired for truth and righteousness, to both tell it and to hear it. The absence of such truth or goodness causes a physiological reaction in our bodies. Researchers suggest that there is the presence of certain involuntary reactions that go on in your body when you are subjected to stressful situations, like telling a lie. Such changes — like heart rate, blood pressure, respiratory rate and electrodermal activity —are detected in a polygraph.

Contrary to popular belief, polygraphs do not detect lies. They detect a difference in the reactions your body has to truth vs. a non-truth or lie. That is why they first ask you questions that determine your truth "baseline." It is then that they are able to notice the physiological responses to statements made contrary to your truth or "baseline."

We also know that a regular diet of bad news and negative situations causes stress. Stress is a killer. It is directly associated with heart disease and cancer, the leading causes of death in the United States. A disease is simply an absolute lack of ease — hence dis-ease.

Stress, toxic environments, and people cause a lack of ease in your heart. Stress is a state of tension that is created when a person responds to the demands and pressures that come from work, family and other external sources, as well as those that are internally generated from self-imposed demands, obligations and self-criticism. All these things rob you of the ease your body requires to function at optimal performance.

Negativity Is Distracting
Researchers say it takes 12 pieces of positive information to overcome one piece of negative information. That's why you go on the Negaholic's Diet. Imagine how much positive you have to take in just to overcome the negative information contained in certain news broadcasts or publications or even the Internet.

Besides being bad for your heart, negative or toxic information serves as a distraction to you reaching your goals and dreams. When you are distracted, you lose focus. This principle works in every area of our

life. The more focused you are, the more effective and productive you will be — just like light. Focused light is laser-beam strong, instead of the weakness of diffused light. If your energy is diffused, you will eventually lose power.

When you're focused, you don't allow yourself to be distracted. Focus does not mean that you abandon your surroundings. You are aware of your surroundings, but you're focused on your objective. Life is too short not be focused to attack your goals with laser-beam precision.

Addiction to the Negative

A scene from the movie Pretty Woman comes to mind. It relates to the effects of taking in bad information. In this scene, Richard Gere's and Julia Roberts' characters were dialoguing about their past relationships, and she tells him about a time when an ex-boyfriend of hers had said some very mean and hurtful things to her. Richard Gere's character asks her why she would believe those things since she is so beautiful. She replies, "Because the bad things are easier to believe."

That is what I call a "negaholic." These are people who are addicted to the negative. They gravitate to it, feed upon it and spread it around. Pessimists often suffer from "negaholism." A negaholic believes that they are simply being realistic — even responsible. Most people who suffer from negaholism do not even realize it. The symptoms are often misdiagnosed as other things. A negaholic's addiction to the negative is often disguised as a concerned citizen who is just seeing things as they really are. Negaholics believe they're simply accepting the facts as they are.

You know that person, the one who, first thing in the morning, turns on the morning news; while reading the morning paper; while checking social media. All in search of bad news. And there is plenty of it if you're looking. Their day would not be complete without their morning dose of negativity. That person is suffering from negaholism. It's an addiction. Some people tell me that they just can't help themselves, but I disagree. You can help yourself and the minute you decide to go on the Negaholic's Diet, you can change your life experience.

A Battle Between Good & Evil

You see, there's a battle between good and evil going on right inside of all of us. There is negativity all around us, and by engaging in it, we simply feed the evil. Focusing on the positive — or the good — strengthens the good inside of you and brings forth more of that. If you don't feed the greedy evil monster, he will eventually starve to death and die away. Negativity will then leave your life.

Realize why soap operas, novellas, and reality shows are so very popular. People watch those shows to feed the need to prove their lives are not that bad. Negativity sells. Newspaper and magazine publishers, TV producers and movie producers all realize that fact. I know reality show stars who have been fired from their own show because their lives did not have enough drama in it. Our society is suffering from Negaholism, and we must eradicate this dis-ease right away.

To eradicate it, you must go on the Negaholic's Diet. This is not about a war on negative but rather a rally for positive. However, if you find yourself addicted to the negative, for the next 30 days, follow the 10 Commandments to Optimistic Living found at www.shelleyroxanne. com. After 30 days on this diet, you're guaranteed to lose the weight of the world.

Shi(f)t Happens

*"You must be the change
you want to see in the world."*
~ Mahatma Gandhi

Embedded within each season is a demand for change. Change is the only constant in life. Adaptability to these changes is critical for success. Effective change is the essence of maturation. Maturity is not about age; it's about accepting responsibility for the situation or circumstance you find yourself in. Own it, without blame or shame and you, will experience the shift.

The reality is, the only work we're ever supposed to do is to work on ourselves. You will not and cannot grow unless you're willing to change. We are that caterpillar going through the process of a metamorphosis. As discussed earlier in the "Break the Shell" chapter, this process is unavoidable if you want to develop, grow and eventually fly. Since change is both inevitable and necessary, it's time you get ready for it when the shift happens.

Change Is a Gift

What most people don't realize is that when change is necessary, not to change is destructive. We find this in every aspect of life. Did you ever notice that you can be on a job that you're perfectly comfortable with and all of a sudden you get fired? That was a gift given to you by the Universe. There was a need for change, and you didn't recognize it, so it had to do that changing for you. Most people who get fired, after some time, of course, always come to the realization that they should have voluntarily left that job long ago, and the termination turned out to be a blessing. If you don't want change to lead you, you'd better get ahead of change and recognize when it's necessary.

> *"I think of life as a good book. The further you get into it,*
> *the more it begins to make sense."*
> ~ Harold Kuschner

Growth is the objective in life, but even positive change can be unnerving. Often with change, even change for the better, a sense of discomfort can come with it. If you have your first child while you're excited about the baby, you may experience a sense of anxiety about the change in responsibility.

If you get a job in a new city, while you're excited about the opportunity, it means you have to change your friends and associates. The same goes for the excitement of getting married; that brings with it the perceived loss of freedom. Change, no matter how good, is going to come, and you might as well welcome it.

Changing Yourself

You're not stuck with who you are. If you don't like what you're seeing, you can change. While you cannot change other people — and you don't need to — you can change yourself. Keep in mind, it's not really you who requires a change; it's the strategy you're using. You are actually perfect just the way you are. Simply modify your strategy if you want to see a successful change in your life experience.

You're looking at the world through your own lenses. Remember, we don't see things as they are, we see them as we are. Like a mirror, the world must project back to you what you project to it. If you don't like what you see in the mirror, don't try to change the mirror, change what is being reflected in the mirror. Therefore, if you believe the world and those around you to be untrustworthy, mean and headed in a wrong direction, check the mirror. Perhaps there are blemishes or flaws you need to address.

Here's a hint… you cannot do anything to change the past so why focus on it. Focusing on your past robs you of your future. Do you realize why the rearview mirror in your car is so small but the front windshield is so large? That is because it's more important where you're going than where you came from. There's no "out there," there is only "in here." Success in your life is an inside job.

"If you are irritated by every rub,
how will your mirror be polished?"
~ Rumi

A First Step — Getting Your Life in Order

Last year I was traveling on a long trip and pulled into a Rest Stop for something to drink. The gas station convenience store was closed, but they had a vending machine outside. I was thirsty and wanted a cold drink. I put the money in the machine, selected my item, and pressed the button. Nothing happened. I shook the machine, kicked it, and banged it trying to force out the item. I then, out of frustration, pressed the lever to get back my change and again nothing happened.

My young son, who was with me, pointed to a small sign on the machine that read "Out-of-Order." I was then reminded of what someone very wise once told me: "Shelley, never invest in something that is out-of-order yet expect change." That vending machine scenario often comes up when I try to help people whose lives are out-of-order.

Until I help them get it back in order, I cannot invest time and energy in helping them reach their life's purpose. First, they must get things in order and then we will see true change and growth. If we don't maintain order, chaos is waiting in the balance. Chaos is a confused, unorganized state. The truth is; things simply work better when they're in order. This includes every area of your life — whether it's order in your relationships, your career, your home, your family, your closet or your own head. Having things in order is critical to your well-being. You've got to clear your mind of all obstruction, which may have been created by wrong thinking.

Personal Clearing Is Powerful

The good news is that there's help for people who are looking to get their lives in order. There are processes available, like personal clearing and

167

space clearing, which are very helpful. There is NLP (Neuro Linguistic Programming), EFT (Emotional Freedom Technique), Meditation, Guided Imagery, and, of course, my personal favorite technique, Prayer. Doing these things can transform your life and change your perspective.

Personal clearing is a powerful tool, and it is something we should make a strong practice. Personal clearing is a way of releasing unwanted mental and emotional patterns. In other chapters, I discuss negative programming that takes place due to past experiences and/or exposure. Personal clearing helps to clear you of the damages of such exposure. It also helps to clear past hurts and negative feelings you have towards anyone who hurt you. Imbalances and disturbances in your body can also be cleared through personal clearing.

I personally have noticed powerful changes to situations in my life after using personal clearing techniques.

"People do not seem to realize that their opinion of the world
is also a confession of character."
~ Ralph Waldo Emerson

Change & Character
Your life will turn around immediately the day you choose to take charge of it. To change, you must make a choice. Your character is at the root of your choices. Therefore, your character determines your destiny. It's your character that sustains everything that you build in life. Therefore, take the time to build your character. Character is to a person what a foundation is to a house. If your life is not built on a firm foundation (strong character), then it will surely fall apart. Your response to issues confronted comes out of your character.

Everyone tries to define this thing called "character." It's not hard. Character is that core essence of your being. It's about your nature. You make decisions out of your character — the imprint of your soul. Character is often defined as how you would be and act if no one was watching. Not to be confused with personality, which people can fake; character cannot be faked. Either you've got strong character, or you don't. Sadly, much less focus is placed upon one's character today than

168

it should be. Character is the very foundation of our lives. I've witnessed far too many people whose skills, talents and abilities have taken them where their character has not sustained them. Be sure to build a strong character. It's the essence of the maturation process.

Remember, maturity comes not with age, but with the acceptance of responsibility for your words, thoughts, motives, and actions. We choose our friends. We choose our spouses. We choose our jobs, our careers, our homes, and our cars. You have no right to complain about who or what you permit into your life by choice. It's not just what you do. It's why you did it. You choose how to live. You're where you are in your life because you chose to be there. Therefore, if you don't like where you are in life, you can change that too. It's time to grow up and put away childish things (ways).

Don't Make Waves in a Kiddie Pool

*"The last of the human freedoms is to choose
one's attitude in any given set of circumstances."*
~ Victor Frankl

My son Evan is very wise; he always has been. Whenever he finds someone making a big deal out of a small one, he says that person is "making waves in a kiddie pool." Just the thought of that makes me laugh. Imagine someone trying to disturb a perfectly peaceful kiddie pool by attempting to make waves in it. This is just plain foolish.

A fool is someone who lacks judgment and prudence. Fools react instead of responding to a situation. People who walk in wisdom think things through. As noted in the last chapter, your life will turn around immediately the day you choose to take charge of it. Walking in wisdom is a great place to start.

Often small things in our lives appear to cast a very large shadow. I recognize that when things are happening to us, they seem to be a very big deal at the time. However, in hindsight, we often look back and laugh at a situation that we thought was a big deal that in retrospect turned out to be nothing at all.

*"Nobody trips over mountains; it is the small pebble that causes you to
stumble. Pass all the pebbles in your path and you will find
that you have crossed the mountain."*
~ Unknown

Don't Sweat the Small Stuff

As author and psychologist Richard Carlson told us, don't sweat the small stuff because it's all small stuff.

Many years ago, I was reminded not to sweat the small stuff. One day as I was passing by my son's bedroom was astonished to see the bed nicely made up and everything neat and tidy. I saw an envelope propped up prominently on the pillow. It was addressed to "Mom." With the worst premonition, I opened the envelope and read the letter with trembling hands…

Dear Mom,

It is with great regret and sorrow that I'm writing you. I had to elope with my new girlfriend because I wanted to avoid a scene with you and Dad. I've been finding real passion with Rose, and she is so nice. I knew you would not approve of her because of all her piercings, tattoos, and her tight motorcycle clothes and because she is so much older than I am. But it's not only the passion, Mom, Rose is pregnant. Rose says that we are going to be very happy together. She rents a trailer in the woods and has a stack of firewood, enough for the entire winter. We share a dream of having many more children. She wants 12. In the meantime, we'll pray that science will find a cure for AIDS so Rose can get better; she sure deserves it!

Don't worry, Mom. I'm 13 years old now, and I know how to take care of myself. Someday, I'm sure we'll be back to visit so you can get to know your grandchildren.

Your son,
Taylor

P.S. Mom, none of the above is true. I'm over at John's house. I just wanted to remind you that there are worse things in life than the report card that's in my top desk drawer. I love you! Call when it's safe for me to come home.

While Taylor is my prankster, he really put things into perspective for me. Taylor is always teaching me not to sweat the small stuff.

The Power to Choose

Most of the stress we experience in life we've created. Our lives right now are exactly how we have chosen them to be, whether we are consciously aware of that or not. We often don't make the necessary changes in our lives unless we are forced to do so. It is the Pleasure vs. Pain Principle.

I realize that it's difficult to admit to the fact that one's difficulties are self-inflicted, but most of the times they are just that. What you are experiencing now in your life is a result of past poor thinking and actions. There is, of course, more good news here. You can change it if you choose to. We always have the power to choose. I refuse to spend my time on the 98% of the things that just don't matter. I will not do it. It's important to fight for the life you want because the life you don't want will show up and take over if you allow it.

Everything is energy. Our physical bodies are energy, our cars are energy, our homes are energy, this book you're reading is energy, money and time are energy. Energy is a resource not to be wasted. Let's say that every morning when you awake, you will be given $1000 worth of energy. Every time you're stressed out, angry or hurt costs you $20 of energy credit. However, each time you apply love and gratitude to situations throughout your day, you gain more energy credits to be used as you please. Would you still spend it the way you are now? Would you still sweat the small stuff? It costs you very deeply, and you cannot afford it. No one can.

Each one of us can choose how we respond to challenging situations in our lives. How we choose to react is a testament to our character. Character is what comes out of us when we are faced with the unexpected. The challenges in our lives expose who we really are.

It's certainly easy to be kind, generous and gentle when things are going well for us. But is it as easy to be generous when we have financial difficulties? Do we give ourselves a pass to be nasty and short with people because we're going through tough times? It's never acceptable to mistreat people.

"Don't forget to show hospitality to strangers, for some who have done this have entertained angels without realizing it"
- Hebrews 13:2

Be Gentle with Others
We're all going through things at different times in our lives, and those are the times when we want people to be gentle with us. It's equally as important to be gentle with others, even when they seem not to deserve it. Your sensitivity and compassion may be just the thing they need to turn their day around for the better.

I am reminded of the story of the middle-aged man who gets on the subway with three rambunctious children. They were unruly, climbing and jumping all over the seats, being disruptive to other passengers on the train. The people around him were annoyed as to why this man just sat there unfazed and despondent while his children caused havoc on the train. People judged him as a negligent father, as someone who didn't discipline his children or care about the comfort of others.

That was all until one curious passenger asked the man a question. "Sir, why are you letting your children act this way?" His response changed everyone's perception when they learned that they had just come from the hospital room where he learned that his wife and their mother had died. Now he was on his way home as a newly single father with no idea how to raise these small children alone. What if they had all known that in advance? Would they have had more compassion and understanding for the man's behavior and that of his children who had just lost their mom?

Realize that you cannot control other people or circumstances that may happen, but you can control your reaction to them. Your attitude will most certainly determine your altitude. Your attitude determines your approach, and your approach determines success.

SECRET 33

Elephants Don't Swat Flies

"Ignore those that make you fearful and sad,
that degrade you back towards disease and death."
~ Rumi

Let's talk a bit about haters. "What are haters?" you ask. Haters are people who for no apparent reason at all dislike you, talk about you, criticize you, are jealous of you, and make you feel bad and sad. But not to worry, haters serve a very valuable purpose in your life. Haters motivate you. Haters fuel you and put that fire under your tuchus (a Yiddish word for buttocks, bottom, or rear end) to keep it moving, or at least they should. The haters in your life are doing exactly what they were put in your life to do. Mediocrity always attacks excellence.

"What do you think a hater's job is? To hate. If you have someone hating on you right now, you better think of how to get five more people hating on you by Christmas. You need haters to make you stronger."
~ Katt Williams, Comedian

How Do You Deal with Haters?
Haters are often like crabs in a barrel. They don't want to see you get ahead — especially if you dare to surpass them and their station in life. Haters drink something called "Hater-aid." It's a bitter drink that keeps them going. So the more you do, the more Hater-aid they drink. Hater-aid is a drink best served iced cold.

What can you do about a hater? Nothing. Haters are going to hate. They're predestined to hate. It's in their DNA. I'm not suggesting that there is no hope for haters. After all, I am an optimist, and I don't believe that anyone is hopeless. But I also believe you shouldn't spend your time trying to change a hater. That's like trying to teach a pig to sing. That does no good. All it does is it wastes your time, and it frustrates the pig. Besides, you're bigger than that. Elephants don't swat flies.

The only way to deal with a hater is by achieving massive success. That's the best revenge. But don't think that this will satisfy the hater. It won't, but it sure will make you feel awesome.

"Anyone can sympathize with the sufferings of a friend,
but it requires a very fine nature to sympathize with a friend's success."
~ Oscar Wilde

When Friends Are Haters

Can your current group of friends sympathize with your success, or are they criticizing you for no apparent reason? When my friend, Alex, purchased his first home, I was so excited for him. The house was large and spacious. It sat on top of a hill with a grand curb appeal. Alex invited his college buddies over to see his new house. He was excited to show them what he had accomplished. Sadly all his "friends" could do was find fault in his slanted backyard and the absence of fencing around the property.

Alex's friends had no idea how their criticism crushed him and deflated his bubble. He thought the accomplishment of a young recent college grad buying his first mini-mansion would be something his friends would celebrate. He had hoped that it would inspire them to want to work hard too. But instead they were just "hating."

Michael Jordan Thanked His Haters

Michael Jordan was inducted into the Basketball Hall of Fame in 2009. The induction speech he gave was — instead of peace, love and happiness and thanking everyone under the sun —about what made him the greatest. He made it a tribute to his haters.

Jordan talked about the 1985 all-star game freeze-out, where jealous older players supposedly stopped passing him the ball. He talked about Pat Riley, a coach who turned basketball into wrestling every time they

played Jordan. He recounted every remark that someone made that he could turn into an insult against him. He used it as fuel. He flew Leroy Smith and Pop Herring in for the ceremony — the player who replaced him on the varsity team, and the coach that "overlooked" him.

He thanked them all. Michael said his friends made him good, but his enemies made him great. It was actually Michael who made up the story — or at least it was his interpretation of the story — about how he got cut from his high-school basketball team. It did not actually happen that way. Apparently Michael was a sophomore and still had some growing to do. So he was passed over by his coach and was not selected for varsity that year. While he did play JV, that was not good enough for Mike. He felt overlooked and slighted. Some may say he had a chip on his shoulder about it, but that chip rode with him all the way to greatness and into the history books.

During this famous speech, Michael Jordan pointed out the guy who made the team "over" him, who was in the audience. He mentioned the NBA vets who froze him out in his first All-Star Game, two of whom were there — George Gervin and Isaiah Thomas. He certainly mentioned Utah Jazz guard Bryon Russell, who was guarding him on his final shot in a Bulls uniform. And, of course, he included former Bulls general manager Jerry Krause, with whom he had real conflict during his career.

Bottom line, he thanked his haters. While others may have thought that Michael did not have to do that, I say, "Good for him." He is a competitor, and he found a way to use his haters to his advantage. Lebron James can also thank his haters. They fueled him to two championship rings for himself and the Miami Heat.

"I'm not offended by all the dumb blonde jokes because I know I'm not dumb. I also know I'm not blonde."
~ Dolly Parton

What the Bible Says
Love your haters. While I was unable, during my research for the book, to find a scripture reference to Haters specifically in the Bible, I was able to find some things that let me know that haters are not a new concept.

177

Of course, we know that Jesus had haters and yet wise men still seek him. But the Word is very clear about how you are to deal with those who hate/persecute you. So here's where it gets good. Not only will you be rewarded for doing good to your enemies, but it also is like pouring hot coals of fire on their heads. Can you say, "Bonus"? It's like the gift that keeps on giving. Sounds like a good deal to me.

Special Advice to the Haters: Never covet what someone else has. Appreciate what you have in your own hand, for out of it will come the things you want in your own life. Again, don't be jealous of what someone else has. You have no idea the price they paid or the sacrifices they made to get it.

"Be who you are and say what you feel, because those who mind don't matter and those who matter don't mind."
~ Dr. Seuss

Jealousy Is a Tribute
Were it not for your haters, you wouldn't even realize how powerful you are. Hey, if you weren't doing anything worth talking about, they wouldn't be talking about you! They'd hate on some other successful person. So do well to your haters by continuing to do big things. Jealousy is the tribute that mediocrity pays to genius.

Let the Good Times Roll

"In all of living, have much fun and laughter.
Life is to be enjoyed, not just endured."
~ Gordon B. Hinckley

We may not be here for a long time, but we are here for a good time. Life is meant to be enjoyed. Enjoy yourself. Most of us enjoy going to amusement parks and carnivals. Why not see your life as an amusement park? It is, after all, a great adventure. There are rides, food and friends and, of course, some scary adventures and clowns. It's all part of the experience.

Enjoying the Camaraderie
As a people watcher, I can find enjoyment in observing people frolic and laugh with friends and family at various events and gatherings. There's nothing more joyous than to watch people having a good time. Sporting events are certainly a place where you can find people gathered, all with a common goal in mind — to have fun. There's nothing more hysterical than to watch grown men painting their bodies, head to toe, in the colors of their favorite team, taking their shirts off, and cheering for 3 hours.

I enjoy being a Sports Mom because I get to be surrounded by extremely talented young people who have the courage to compete and pursue their dreams. There's a certain sadness that occurs when a season ends — be it football, basketball, swimming, track or whatever sport you choose to enjoy. That's because the camaraderie that occurs amongst the people enjoying that sporting event together ends, at least until the next season.

Summer had always been my favorite season because that's when

179

I had the most fun – as a child, anyway. Besides Christmas, the summer season was when people were the most jovial and happy. It seemed there was a party or barbecue every weekend. You got to go to the beach, swim in the pool, and enjoy outdoor activities. People just seemed to be less uptight and more open to life during the summer season.

"Don't make fun and enjoyment an option, make them a priority."
~ Aine Belton

Join the Party!
One of my many business ventures was that of an event planner. I have been planning events since I was in the sixth grade. We used to have a small house on our property where I grew up, and that was where "Shelley's parties" would take place. It was a very tiny house, but it had everything we needed, including a dance floor and a bathroom – the basics for making a great event. Shelley's parties were the talk of the town.

So much so, that at my 20th-year class reunion, people were still talking about my parties. The key to being a great event planner is ensuring that it be about your guests and not about you. It's important to see to it that your guests feel well taken care of and are having a good time. That's the secret to a great party.

Even Jesus knew the benefits of a great party. He turned water into wine so that the guests at a wedding could keep the party going. The funny part about this story is that His wine turned out to be better than the wine the host initially served. Now, if having a good time were not important, it would not have been covered in the Bible. Frankly, that event is where Jesus performed his first recorded miracle. As an event planner, I have certainly had to turn water into wine a few times, so I can relate!

The Best Is Yet to Come
This message became my mantra as I traveled the nation spreading my message of optimism. Each time I sign off Optimistic Radio, I sign off with those words – the best is yet to come. That doesn't mean that you are

to live in the future awaiting some better time. Simply by virtue of stating "the best" is yet to come means in and of itself that good, even great, is already here, and if you like this, well then the best is yet to come. No matter your age, your best days are still ahead of you.

There was a client of mine who would constantly talk about the good times in his life. He would reminisce about the good ol' days. The only problem was, those times were always in the past. Not even the recent past, but the distant past. He spoke of times when he was in college. He gave a level of detail to the stories as if those events happened yesterday.

But in actuality, it was 35 years ago! I couldn't believe that when he recalled a fun time in his life, he had to go back so far into his past. He was enduring his life since then, not enjoying it.

Can you recall the last time you had fun? Please don't go back 35 years. I hope you don't have to go back any further than yesterday – truly yesterday. Not the one that "feels like" yesterday, the real yesterday. Preferably you can say that you're having a good time right now reading this book. I certainly hope so.

Enjoyment without Guilt
Don't feel guilty about enjoying yourself. Life was designed for just that purpose. Life is not meant to be endured as if you're in captivity, waiting to be set free. What would be the point of it all if you simply had to endure life? Sure, it has its ups and down. But if your approach is right, the downs can be few and far between, and you can still enjoy the ride with confidence that it keeps getting better. Don't sabotage the good times worrying about the bad ones to come. That other shoe may never drop.

Know When to Leave the Party

*"All you have to do is to pay attention; lessons always
arrive when you are ready, and if you can read the signs,
you will learn everything you need to know
in order to take the next step."*
~ Paulo Coelho

This principle was inspired by my friend Eddie Harris. Well, actually it was Eddie's mom. You see, when Eddie was a young man, he was quite the social guy. He was a good-looking man with a lot of charisma. Eddie was the life of the party. He was in a band, and you know what happens when you're a good-looking young guy in a band. Let's just say, you get a lot of attention and have a lot of options.

Whenever Eddie went out for the night, his mother would always tell him, "Eddie, know when to leave the party." This was such profound advice for her to give to her son, as it was for me when he shared it with me. Knowing when to leave the party is a valuable principle for our lives. Eddie's mom was likely telling him to be aware of his surroundings and to know when it was time to get out of a potentially compromising situation at a club or gathering.

More to This Mom's Profound Advice
Knowing when to leave the party also means to know when to leave a job or even a profession, or to know when to leave a relationship or even a city. What I know for sure is that if you stay somewhere longer than you are supposed to, you put yourself in a potentially dangerous position. When change is necessary, not to change is destructive.

At one point in my life, I was in an industry that was very lucrative. Things were going well in the business, and most of my colleagues thought this would last forever. But there was something in my gut that told me it was time to get out, and I listened. Thank God, I did. Shortly after leaving that industry, a tsunami came through that entire business arena leaving nothing but debris and broken promises in its wake. I was glad that I knew when to leave the party.

I had heard stories of people who didn't know when to leave the party and stayed longer than they should have. It ended up costing them their money, freedom and sometimes their lives.

Pay Attention to the Signs

We are always given signs. It's up to us to choose to ignore the signs or to pay close attention to them early on. The earlier we pay attention to the signs, the better off we will be. Imagine traveling down an unfamiliar road. Road signs begin to appear indicating yield or caution. There may even be flashing yellow lights. There may even be other cars headed towards you flashing their headlights in an effort to warn you of what is ahead, and yet you ignore the signs.

You get farther down the road only to find there is a police officer hiding in the bushes waiting to give you a ticket. If you get a ticket, count it as joy because it was possibly saving you from something far worse. What you didn't know is that the next sign would be huge, and it would say, "Road ends." There are always signs. The universe is designed that way. No loving God would allow you to walk into danger without warnings – multiple ones. It's up to us to pay attention to the signs and to take the appropriate action.

Rarely Are We Blind-sided

As a Human Resource Executive, I had a warning system in which to alert employees when their performance required improvement. When I was in Employee Relations, sometimes a manager of a department wanted to fire someone. I would have to ensure that the employee was given the proper warnings. This way, no employee could come to me and say they had no idea that their performance or behavior was unacceptable. We had a way of documenting that the employee was properly warned.

Although we may want to appear to be blind-sided by life, in actuality we never really are. There are always signs.

184

When a relationship goes bad, you may be surprised, even saddened, by its ending. However, usually you are not shocked, or at least you shouldn't be. If you're indeed shocked, that is because you didn't pay attention to the signs. In most cases, a marriage or even a friendship falls apart long before the relationship has a formal ending. If you paid attention to the signs, you would see that either you or the other person began to indicate an unhappiness or displeasure with the way things were going – if not in words than in deeds. If the relationship is important to you, never ignore the early warning signs. As the Jackson 5 told us, we may save a love in our life that we cherish by stopping and paying attention.

Listen to the Still Small Voice
There was a woman who normally traveled with her two friends to get to work at the World Trade Center in New York City. Every day they would carpool to work together. But on September 11, 2001, this woman developed a very bad nose bleed when getting ready for work. She was disturbed and upset because she didn't like to miss work. Her girlfriends came to her house to pick her up, and she told them to go on ahead without her because she needed to deal with the bleeding. She did everything to try to get to work that day, but something told her to stay at home. Later on, she learned that both her girlfriends perished in the tragedy of the World Trade Center. But she was spared.

There are tons of stories just like that one about that particular day. Several people missed their flight or missed their train or bus that day or were for some other reason delayed. And that delay caused them to miss the tragedy. They were spared. I spoke personally with a woman who had an argument with her husband on the morning of September 11th. She said she knew better not to let him leave the house angry, but she was stubborn and let him go. Something told her to make up with him before he left, but she ignored her gut feeling. Sadly, her husband was one of the people to perish in the tragedy that day. His widowed wife will always regret not paying attention to that still small voice inside of her and making up with her husband that fateful morning. She missed the opportunity to let him know how much he was loved before he went off to work that day.

Break the Rules
When I was 18 years old, one Friday night, I went to a drive-in movie theater with my uncle and his best friend. The three of us rode together in my uncle's cute sporty car. His best friend rode in the passenger seat while I sat in the back on our way to the drive-in. Normally my protocol is to leave an event or party with the same people I came there with. But this particular night, I broke the rules.

For some reason, I decided to ride home with a girl from my class. This girl was not a close friend of mine. While I knew her from school, we didn't hang out before that night or after. But something told me to ride home with her after the movie instead of going back with my uncle and his friend. I told my uncle – much to his chagrin – that I was going home with someone else. I assured him that she would drive me straight home. And she did.

Later that night I was awoken by my parents who told me that my uncle and his best friend had been in a horrible car accident. My uncle's best friend had been killed. My uncle survived the accident, but his arm was seriously damaged in the crash. My parents took me to see the remains of what was once the car that we rode in that fateful night. It didn't look like a car; it actually looked more like a motorcycle because all that was left was the driver's seat. The entire frame was gone, as was the passenger side where my uncle's best friend sat. The entire back seat where I had sat was also completely gone.

I listened to the still small voice and for that reason I'm here to tell you about it.

Early Detection Saves Lives
Let's say you drive to work the same way every day. Then, for some reason, you're urged to go a different way one day. Do it. Don't fight it. You may be saved from a situation that is potentially dangerous. Trust that voice inside of you that's guiding you to safety. My mother used to love country artist Kenny Rogers. She played his song "The Gambler" so much I thought it would run the grooves out of the record. But my

favorite part of that song was the chorus when he sang about knowing what to do with your cards and knowing when to walk away or run. It was great advice.

We all hear the advice of the medical community who tell us about how early detection when it comes to our physical health, can save your life. Well, the same goes for the rest of our lives too. Pay attention to the signs early because early detection can save your life.

Return Empty

*"When I stand before God at the end of my life,
I would hope that I would not have a single bit of talent
left, and could say, 'I used everything you gave me.'"*
~ Erma Bombeck

We brought nothing into the world, and it's certain that we can carry nothing out of it. No matter how much "stuff" you acquire along your journey, you can't take it with you to the next place. What good will your money be to you once you transition, no matter where you think you are going after this? What good will your skills, talents and abilities be to you at the next level? Why not use them up now? You can't even save your skills, talents and abilities and pass them on to your loved ones. If you don't use them, you lose them.

Are You Using All Your Gas?
Each time I travel and get a rental car, they ask me the same question. Will you be returning this full or empty? They let you know that if you return it full, it costs less. But, if you return it without a full tank, they will have to fill it up there, and you end up paying a premium for the gas you used. Your life can be compared to that of a rental car. No matter what it costs you, ride it until the wheels fall off, and return it on "E" (Empty).

When your life is all over, you should have no regrets. The worst three words anyone can say at the end of their journey is could've, should've or would've. I've interviewed people who work for hospice and other groups that do the wonderful work of nurturing people who are knowingly at the end of their journey. The overwhelmingly popular thing that they all say is how those people, at the end of their lives, expressed their regrets. Never did they regret not spending enough time at the office or having worked on a job harder. Most often the regrets were about how they spent their "gas."

If they had it to do all over again, most say they would have spent more time enjoying the journey. They would have taken more risks. They would have worried less and laughed more. They would have spent more time with their children and other loved ones. They would have lived fearlessly. I certainly plan to return this rental on E.

On Getting Older

I'm turning 50 at the same time as some of the coolest people on the planet. Lenny Kravitz, Sandra Bullock, Michelle Obama, Stephen Colbert, Wanda Sykes, Stone Cold Steve Austin, Russell Crowe, Elle Macpherson and Cedric the Entertainer. From hilariously funny people to rock stars to supermodels and even the First Lady - I am in a distinguished class of people and am honored to be here. I'm not sure why our society has such a fascination with youth and the search for some fountain. Aging is an inevitable process that we all must grow through - if you are lucky. It seems to be an oxymoron.

On one had we'd hate to see someone die at 60, saying they were far too young, yet while they are alive we make them feel old. What is the alternative? There is something to say for things that are aged. Aged meats are more expensive and more valued. They tend to be more savory, tender and tasty. God forbid that we drink a wine before its time or eat a cheese that has not been matured. Why don't we have the same approach with people? It's hypocrisy. At one point, I was caught up in the deception of not appreciating my age. I was probably 37 for about five years. I remember even throwing myself a 35th birthday party, but the invitation called it the 5th anniversary of my 30th birthday. But now as I reflect, the wisdom I have gained over these 50 years is priceless and invaluable. I wouldn't for one-second trade the wisdom I've gained to be younger than this. I feel alive and rich and confident and beautiful and sexy and smart and wise and talented. Why would I ever give that up for insecurity, uncertainty, ignorance, and low-self-esteem?

That is just insanity. Before this I just thought I was all of those things, now it is what I know for sure. I understand what Dr. Maya

Angelou meant when she said - "I wouldn't give nothing for my journey now." I've graduated to a class few ever get to and I've earned my matriculation. The first 50 years I was learning me, and the next fifty years I am doing me. The problem is most people want to "do them" without first learning themselves, and you cannot do it in that order.

You are on a national treasure hunt to find out who you are. That takes a significant amount of time. If you avoid conducting the search then the later you have to enjoy the treasure when you discover it.

In this short time - and 50 years is a short time in the scheme of things - I've seen my mother pass away suddenly and my favorite cousin and my best friend - neither of whom made it to 50, transition far too soon. While I sincerely miss the physicality of these wonderful woman, it was in their deaths that I learned how to live. I've examined each of their lives and learned what to do - and what not to do - in order to live my life better.

So now, I am living for Glo, and Michelle and Dumpsey and it is through me that they shall live on. Although, I wish they were here to see me now, I know that they are right here beside me - my cheering squad - cheering me on all the way yelling'...You go girl.

"Don't die with your music still in you."
- Wayne Dyer

At the end of this journey for you, will you be left with gas still in the tank or songs left unsung? I hope you will have used all of the potential inside of you. I've witnessed too many people, of all ages, dying on "F" (Full). Due to low self-esteem, peer pressure, fear or more, they simply didn't use what was given to them.

Many are afraid to use up their resources, thinking they may somehow run out. Not only is that selfish, I believe that we need to work on your faith. You are actually given all you will need to enjoy the ride. Don't die with gas left in your tank.

Don't Withhold – Your Supply Is Unlimited
If you're one who believes that you have to "save up" for the journey,

it's obvious that you are under the assumption that there are limitations and lack in your world. It's a deception. Don't buy it. The Universe has an unlimited source of all you will need to get through this journey being the highest and best expression of yourself. You could not possibly use up all the potential resident inside of you.

If you're still here – no matter how old or young – there's more left in the tank. Use it all up, no matter the costs. Buckle up and enjoy the ride!

PART.SiX

RELATIONSHIP
WITH
OTHERS

SECRET 37

Beware of the Company You Keep

"Surround yourself with optimistic people."
~ Zig Ziglar

The relationships you have at this stage are an important factor in how quickly you reach your goals. Stay away from dream killers. Stay around those who celebrate you and not just tolerate you. To be tolerant of someone means that you don't want to deal with them, but you feel you have to for some reason or another. We shouldn't even be teaching tolerance. It seems it's just a way to get people to put up with each other. We need to do better than that. For it is written that evil companionship corrupts good behavior.

Listen, I don't know about you, but I have no desire to spend my time around people who simply tolerate me. I need people around me who celebrate me. This is not about ego; this is about the fact that it's not beneficial to society as a whole to have a bunch of people simply tolerating each other. We need people celebrating each other. Again, I'm talking about being authentic. Not just "blowing smoke" or "hyping" people. I mean truly lifting each other up with encouragement and recognition. Allowing people to be exactly who they are. I'm at my best when I can shine my light as bright as possible.

Therefore, if I'm around people who do not require that I dim my light to make them more comfortable, then I can also hold up the light for them too. It benefits everyone if you can be at your best and brightest. There were times in my life when I received promotions or recognition for my accomplishments, and I couldn't share it with the people closest to me – at that time – all because they weren't happy with themselves. So they could not, or would not, express happiness for me.

I perform better when I'm surrounded by people who make me want to be my best. That only happens when they're bringing their best to the table as well. If you make me want to be a better me, than we can hang out.

Your Destiny Is Tied to Your Relationships
I've heard it said that if you hang out with people who limp, you will eventually develop a limp. Remember, habits are contagious.

Consider this story
A young man named Ricky was 16 years old and very bright and in-telligent. He got great grades in school, and his teachers recognized his potential. The problem was that the crew of kids Ricky hung out with didn't believe that smart kids were cool. So Ricky began cutting class, acting out, and not handing in his school work because he didn't want to be perceived as un-cool by his friends. Ricky then got poor grades, bad report cards, and detention for his behavior – just to fit in with his crew. I wish Ricky's story was unique, but it's not, especially in certain neighborhoods.

I wish I could grab every "Ricky-type" of child and let them know they're making such a grave decision by dimming their bright light just to fit in. How many of you know a Ricky? Are you a Ricky? Do you dim your light to make others feel comfortable around you or to fit in with a crowd? Sadly, Ricky's story does not end there; I wish it did. Not long after Ricky's grades took a turn, he qualified to hang out with this certain crew.

One night, he went out for what he believed to be a joy ride with some friends. They stopped at a convenience store for snacks. Ricky held the door open as one of his buddies foolishly decided to steal something from the store. Although Ricky was not privy to the plan, his friends were actually robbing the store that night. Because of the company he kept, Ricky was caught on surveillance cameras and was arrested with the rest of the crew. Because of the laws in the particular state that Ricky lives in, he is now serving a life sentence in a federal prison, just for choosing the wrong company. This may be unjust and even extreme, but the reality is you are judged by the company you keep.

Ricky was not a bad kid, but he chose bad company, and that was enough to derail his chances at a great life. Keeping the wrong company can lead you to dislocation. Dislocation is when you're removed from the environment and relationships intended to help you fulfill your purpose. Ricky's story is a perfect example of this point. Dislocation leads to destruction and ruin. Yikes! You don't want that, do you? If you're spending time with the wrong crowd, they're standing in the way of you getting to the right crowd. Pull out and step up. Then you can be seen by the right people, who are willing to go where you want to go, and help you get there.

> *"Do not stray onto the path of wicked people.*
> *Do not walk in the way of evil people. Avoid it. Do not walk near it.*
> *Turn away from it and keep walking."*
> ~ Proverbs 4:14-15

Don't complain about who or what you allow into your life. You attracted them there by who and what you are. If you want to attract better people, be a better person.

Competing vs. Inspiring

Jealousy manifests itself in the spirit of competition. This is another indication when you may be hanging around with the wrong people. There is a big difference between allowing someone's life to inspire you and trying to keep up with the Joneses. By the way, who are the Joneses anyway? What I found is that the Joneses are trying to keep up with the Joneses also.

When Jeff and I purchased our first home, our neighbors would look to see what we would do with the house, and they would try to outdo us with bigger or better things. When we put in a pool, they put in a bigger one. When we put up a fence, they put up a taller one. When we put in landscaping with plants, they planted trees. It became exhausting to watch.

Surely they were not able to be creative because they were focused upon competition. Don't try to compete with other people. Do you. There is enough good to go around. I respect the people who can compliment something you have and even ask for your advice on how they can get something similar. That is fine. As they say, imitation is the greatest form of flattery. But when that imitation becomes competition, I believe it prohibits you from being creative and from being your best self.

As Dr. Wayne Dyer told us, inspiration is your ultimate calling. You should be giving inspiration in all you do and finding inspiration in all you see. Just make sure to put your spice on it and don't be afraid to let the person know that they have inspired you. It will mean a lot to them; trust me.

A Circle of Support

Many years ago, early in our relationship Jeff and I were in a major international network marketing organization. We spent several years in this fine association. To this day, I believe it was the absolute best experience for us as a young couple. I highly recommend being a part of a Network Marketing Organization (NMO), if you're looking for a group of people who will celebrate you and support you. They like to boast that you're in business for yourself but not by yourself. And that is so true.

Now, don't get this confused with a "pyramid scheme" or some illegal dealings, although I must say the camaraderie does resemble a gang. I never before had seen groups of people who were so positive and cooperative with each other. Even people from "cross line" organizations who don't directly benefit from your success are so amazingly supportive and helpful. Nowhere else will people in the same business as you teach you exactly what they did to rise to the level of success that you aspire to reach.

Once during our tenure in this particular NMO, I broke my leg during our move from one house to another. I had three small children, two who were under 14 months old at the time. I was overwhelmed and in need of some help. My closest and dearest friends did not offer at all to help me.

On the other hand, women from the Network Marketing

Organization led by Eddie and Elise Vicinanza, not even in our direct upline (which means these people did not directly benefit from the success of our organization nor was there any financial gain for helping me) offered to help me move into my new home. Even to the point where Elise told me, "Just sit down, put your leg up, and simply point where you want things to go, and we will do it for you."

That was years ago, and I still get misty at the thought of these wonderful women offering to help me when my "so-called friends" didn't bother. At that time, I was breastfeeding an infant and had a one-year-old toddler to tend to as well. With a baby on each hip, a full cast on my leg and boxes everywhere, were it not for my mother, my mother-in-law, and great people like that, I don't know what I would have done. One of the things I've learned along this journey is that I don't need a certain number of friends; I just need friends I can be certain of.

Eddie and Elise unselfishly stood in the gap for Jeff and me without any benefit to themselves. They invited us into their business family and treated us as one of their own. We will forever be grateful and continue to pay it forward.

A Lift Up or a Push-Down?
Eddie V. always taught us that it was best to associate with people at your level and above. It was in that organization that I learned the importance of associating with the right people. People at your level are simply people who share your right thinking. Because if their thinking is right, their results are right. Conversely, if their thinking is broke, their results are broke.

If you're the smartest person in your group, find another group. You need to surround yourself with people who challenge you to be a better person... to step up your game. Michael Jordan is arguably the best basketball player ever to play the game. He won multiple championships because he made those around him step up their game and reach higher... literally. I have some actor friends who say that when they perform with a great actor, it makes them a better actor.

As iron sharpens iron, so one man sharpens another. If you want to remain optimistic, you must surround yourself with optimistic people.

Lord knows, that negativity is contagious.

You are affected and infected – either positively or negatively – by the company you keep. They will bring you down before you bring them up. Beware.

TEST: Ask yourself – If you knew your destiny was tied to your relationships, would you be willing to put your destiny in the hands of the people in your circle? Would you trust them with your life and future?

To find out where you're going, just look at who's driving the bus that you're on and who's on that bus. Clearly, this is a prediction of your future.

Check Your Relationship Accounts

"Some people find fault like there is a reward for it."
~ Zig Ziglar

Our relationships can be compared to bank accounts. When we are able, we should be making regular deposits of goodness, kindness, encouragement, support and love into our relationship accounts. This way, if you ever need to go to the account to make a withdrawal, your request will not come up marked "insufficient."

Have you checked the balance on your relationship accounts lately? If you're wondering why your requests for love, encouragement and support are coming up short and bouncing back, maybe you haven't made enough deposits to cover the withdrawal you are trying to make now. Don't try to go continually to an account to which you have not made the sufficient deposits attempting to make withdrawals. Be sure to keep the (relationship) account in good standing. Therefore, there will be a sufficient amount on deposit to cover your request.

"Our prime purpose in this life is to help others.
And if you can't help them, at least don't hurt them."
~ Dalai Lama XIV

Pay It Forward
It's often your time and not your money that is needed by others. Anyone can give (deposit) money but no one can give (deposit) specifically what you can, and that is you. If you are impacting your society, then your absence will create a void. If you are absent, and no one misses you, you

need to check to see if you are making the right impact. If it's your goal to find greatness in this life, then find a way to serve people. It is in the service of others that you find your greatness. That is the rent you pay for enjoying a great life.

I'm sure if you were tasked with thinking of the times when you felt the most blessed; it was when someone did something special for you. When they gave of themselves in a way that only they could do. I'd bet that when you felt the most loved and taken care of, you felt your most powerful. It wasn't your mother's money that made you feel better when you were sick. It was her tucking you into bed, or making you hot soup, or just holding you safely in her arms. Those were great deposits she made into your life. Or maybe it was Grandma or Nana who was supportive of you – no matter what you wanted to do – that made you feel unstoppable. Grandma was making deposits.

Well, it's time to pay it forward. If you have a desire to do great things in the world and to live a great life, make special deposits in the life of others.

A Gift Better Than Money

There's always something you can do for others. "The Story of Peter and the Beggar" – I call it "The Beautiful Story" – is the best example to make my point. The story says:

One day, Peter and John were going up to the temple to pray. Now a man who was lame from birth was being carried to the temple gate called Beautiful, where he was put every day to beg from those going into the temple courts. When he saw Peter and John about to enter, he asked them for money. Peter looked straight at him and said, "Look at us!" So the man gave them his attention, expecting to get something from them.

Then Peter said, "Silver or gold I do not have, but what I do have I give you. In the name of Jesus Christ of Nazareth, walk." Taking him by the right hand, Peter helped the lame beggar up, and instantly the man's feet and ankles became strong. He jumped to his feet and began to walk. Then he went with Peter and John into the temple courts, walking and jumping, and praising God. When all the people saw him walking

and praising God, they recognized him as the same guy who used to sit begging at the temple gate called Beautiful, and they were filled with wonder and amazement at what had happened to him. The man threw his arms around Peter and John because he was ecstatic. (Acts 3:1-11)

It was not Peter's and John's money that helped the man. Had they given him money, it would have only changed his situation temporarily. Instead, they gave him something more powerful. They gave him the gift of an encouraging word. They told him that although they did not have money to give him, they could be of service to him in another way. They instead gave him something far greater; they gave him of their substance, the power to heal. This deposit was of much greater benefit than any silver or gold that they could have given him.

The Joy Questionnaire

Leo Buscaglia was a best-selling author of inspirational books on the subjects of love and the meaning of life. He suggested that Ancient Egyptians believed that upon death they would be asked two questions, and their answers would determine whether they could continue their journey in the afterlife. The first question was "Did you bring joy?" The second was "Did you find joy?"

At the end of your days, how will you answer these questions? I can guarantee you that serving and depositing into the lives of others accomplishes both these two charges. You end up bringing joy and finding joy at the same time, in the act of service. Now that's are true return on investment.

My Mom & Dad - Great Role Models

I had great examples of what it means to be of service to others in my mother and father. My dad is a Rotarian. The main tenet of Rotary International is "Service above Self." My parents were an example of living that tenet my entire life.

As a young girl, I would often wake up to find a strange child lying in the bed next to me that my parents unselfishly took in during the night. If someone was distressed and needed a safe, loving place to stay, my parents provided it. Although I only have one biological sibling, I have lots of "bonus" brothers and sisters who were raised alongside me at my parent's house. Years would pass, and my "bonus" siblings would still be there, getting all the love and attention my brother and I got without distinction.

Recently my father was honored by one of the many organizations that he has dedicated his life to serving. While working with the designers to develop his biography, we literally had to edit down all of the groups and organizations that he volunteered with because we ran out of space in the journal. To this day, he serves on multiple boards, usually serving as chairman without any compensation whatsoever.

Where did he find the time? He gave to the community in public service, to the church in reverence, and to his family in love. Never did I feel slighted or that he did not have enough love left over for me. Instead, I was inspired by the example that both my parents provided by being lifelong depositors. Neither one of my parents possessed a selfish bone in their bodies. It's for this reason if they ever needed to go to their relationship accounts to make a withdrawal, the account would be fully sufficient to cover the demand.

Mom and Dad found such joy in serving other people. Therefore, if Glo was asked the questions, like the Ancient Egyptians were asked, upon her transition, "Did you bring joy… did you find joy?" Glo could answer both of those questions with a loud resounding YES.

It Pays to Be Nice

*"Be kind, for everyone you meet is
fighting a hard battle."*
~ John Watson

When we moved from one school district to another, my son Taylor was sad to be leaving his friends in his old school. Both he and Myles were very popular in their school and had developed great relationships there. As a parent who understands the importance of building self-esteem in your children, I recognized how crucial establishing good relationships are to having a great school experience.

Mom Gets an Idea

At one point throughout that new school year, I saw that Taylor needed some encouragement. He needed reassurance that the kids in his class did in fact like him, although they may not have shown it all the time. In middle school, kids can be so mean, as many have not yet developed the skill of saying nice things to each other – even if they mean to do this.

So I went to the bank and got 27 brand new shiny $2 bills. It was Taylor's birthday, and when the boys were in school, especially in the early years, I always liked to get their classmates involved in the celebration of my sons' birthdays.

Once when Evan turned six years old, I stuffed this curvy body into a body-hugging suit and dressed up like a Power Ranger – helmet and all. I went to a professional costume shop and rented the official red Power Ranger costume. Then I went to Evan's school, in 95-degree weather no less, dressed as Jason the Red Power Ranger, to entertain all the children in the entire school in celebration of Evan's birthday.

But for this particular birthday for Taylor, I decided to do something different for him. So I went to his classroom and fanned out all the shiny new $2 bills. I stood in the front of the class and posed the question, "Who wants this money?" As you can imagine, every kid raised their hand and nearly charged at me in the front of the room to get it. "OK, OK," I said, "Calm down." I told the class, "I will give a brand new $2 bill for each one of you that has something nice to say about Taylor today. As an added bonus, you will speak this over the microphone, and your voice will be broadcast on-the-air on the radio for everyone to hear what nice things you have to say."

I went around the classroom with a mic and recorded each child as they gave Taylor wonderful accolades and kind words. As they said something kind, I gave them their $2 bill, and went on to the next child and then to the next child and so on until everyone had something to say. Even the teacher got involved, and she too had great things to say about Taylor. Little did I know what great lessons that offered for all of us that day.

The Lessons
First, it proved to the children that it paid to be nice. Second, I was astounded how easy it was to get children to find something nice to say about someone that they really didn't even know that well. Kids told Taylor was awesome with a capital A and some even talked about his smile and about how he made them laugh because he was so funny. It warmed my heart so much to hear that my children were acting as fine ambassadors of good will in their own worlds.

But the most rewarding part is that although I was giving the money in exchange for a kind word, many of the children gave the kind word but refused to take the money. They were so happy about how it felt to be doing something nice that they didn't want to take the money for doing what should have been done already. You see, I set out to do one thing but in exchange I accomplished something far greater. I learned just how precious people really are at all ages. Kids are not mean, they just haven't been taught how to be nice. They just needed to be properly incentivized and then given the opportunity to do what's right.

Taylor's self-esteem needed lifting and the gift for his birthday was to give to his classmates, and sure enough they gave genuinely back to him, and me, in a beautiful tribute that he will treasure forever – as will I. To this day, we listen to that recording, and I know he is uplifted by the great things his classmates had to say about him. I did air that on the radio as promised and again the gift just kept on giving.

People were inspired all over the world to go around giving encouraging words to each other. Money just happened to be an initial motivator for the children. But once the children learned how it felt to be kind to each other, the motivator wasn't necessary anymore. Those young children are now young adults, and I often hear from them how that day really changed their perspective and their outlook. Honestly, that was not my goal but it sure was a great benefit. It truly pays to be nice.

You Are Your Brother's Keeper

"Never drive faster than your guardian angel can fly."
~ Unknown Author

Am I my brother's keeper? I was shocked when I asked this question to my listening audience during a recent Shelley Roxanne Show. I was surprised to find out how many people actually answered "no" to this question. I've got news for you. You are your brother's keeper, and your brother is your keeper. We are indeed responsible to our fellow man.

A Type of Buddy System

This concept can get somewhat controversial. Some feel they have a hard enough time dealing with their own difficulties and challenges, and that they have no time for anyone else's. Meanwhile, it's a fact that what I do can affect you and vice versa. So it would make sense that you would benefit from me doing well, and I would benefit from your well-being too.

To each of us, there should be at least someone to look out for us. We each should have a keeper. Not necessarily a biological brother but someone who's a witness to our lives, someone responsible for loving on us and telling us when we're going in a wrong direction. Someone to celebrate us and remind us of our goodness. Each time I see a homeless person or a beggar, I ask myself, Where is his brother? Where is the person responsible for looking out for that guy? Kind of like a buddy system, we are accountable to someone and them to us. For example, if you have a spouse, that person is a witness to your life. They are your keeper, and you are theirs. Maybe it's a friend or a sibling.

Everyone needs someone to love and someone to receive love back. People who feel loved could not, would not, commit some of the heinous acts that we see today because love would not permit it. Imagine how different our world would be if our brothers were doing their jobs. How many senseless tragedies could be prevented if we were our brother's keeper and took that job seriously?

We Don't Live in This World Alone

You can certainly get a dose of how we affect each other on even a less serious scale, like when you're stuck in traffic due to an accident on the road. Often it's not serious. The bottleneck may be due to what is called "rubber-necking."

This occurs when people slow down to see what's going on over on the side of the road. I've seen car pileups for miles and miles due to a fender bender. I've thought to myself that the two people who were involved in that fender bender affected the lives of thousands of people, albeit not intentionally. That crash between those two drivers caused thousands of people to be late getting to work or caused them to miss other engagements, which they were headed to prior to getting stuck in traffic.

> *"The richest man on the earth is the one*
> *with his last friend, not his first dollar."*
> ~ Unknown

Our recent history has proved our need for keepers. Over the past few years, there have been numerous school shootings in which one student randomly turned a gun on innocent bystanders. After shooting up the school, injuring some and killing more, he then turns the gun on himself. All I could think of in that situation is where was his keeper at that time?

Was there no one who saw that this kid needed help? People dismiss these kids as weird and introverted. Perhaps if someone took the time to care about their well-being, it would save a lot of lives later on. Am I suggesting it was anyone's fault except the gunman? No. But I am

210

suggesting that we are affected by the decisions that other people make. We don't live in this world by ourselves. In many ways, we are all deeply connected. Just like one body.

When I stubbed my toe, my entire body hurt – not just the toe. At times, it may seem as if something bad is happening to someone else, and it doesn't affect us – but that's untrue. They are a part of us and us of them. It is our responsibility to take care of each other. If you win, we all win. That's why I want to help you win so that I can win too.

We Could Use Friends Like These

One of the most vivid stories of brother's keepers comes from the "self-help book" in Mark 2:1-12. You need to find keepers like the ones this man had in Mark's Chapter 2. This man was in need of help. He had an emergency and needed it addressed right away. He was unable to help himself. But his four crazy friends would not let an obstacle stop them from getting help for their brother. These guys would not be deterred. They were doing their job as their brother's keeper. As the story goes, when they were trying to get to the house where Jesus was appearing, they had to carry their friend, a paralyzed man, through a large crowd of people who were also trying to get into the house.

At this point, Jesus was like the rock stars are today. He was very popular, and huge crowds gathered every time the word got out that he was going to be in their area. That reminds me of when I left my house at three o'clock in the morning because I heard Ricky Martin was in town, and I went to see him. But I digress… This man's keepers carried him, pushing their way through the crowd. But when they approached the house, it was far too crowded to get in. There were so many people that no one could get in or out. They had a problem. They were unable to gain access through the door. Most people would have given up at that point.

These keepers could have told their friend, "Listen, we're sorry. We tried to help you, but we can't get in. It's sold out. The bouncers at the door will not let anyone else in." But they didn't do that. They loved their brother and were determined to get him some help. So they decided the only way into the house was through the roof. Somehow, these crazy guys climbed up the side of the house, all the while they were carrying their friend. I still don't know how they managed to climb up onto the roof of this house carrying the man and did not drop him. But they did not abandon the plan when it got challenging. Instead, they got creative.

The challenge did not stop at the climbing up onto the roof. They then had to figure out how to get their friend inside the house. So they dug through the roof tiles and found a way to cut a hole in the roof large enough to get the man through. Then together they had to hoist their paralyzed, immobilized, debilitated friend down through the ceiling into the house where they believed he would get help. Now those were some crazy friends.

They risked getting arrested, stoned or whatever other punishment would accompany them crashing the event and cutting through the host's home just to get their brother some help. I want those kinds of keepers, the kind that don't stop at the first obstacle or the second or the third. They looked after him until they were able to get him well again. Now that's what I call brother's keepers.

He's Your Brother

If everyone were to be each other's keeper, no one would be unsafe or uncared for. Each of us would have someone looking out for us – no matter who we are. Wouldn't that be awesome? In the end, he ain't heavy, he's my brother.

Give What You Need

"There is a wonderful mythical law of nature that the three things we crave most in life – happiness, freedom and peace of mind – are always attained by giving them to someone else."
~ Peyton Conway March

Giving is back in style. People all over the world are catching the fever and realizing the personal benefits of giving. Give to others the very things you need most in your life, be it forgiveness, time, money, love or friendship, because whatever you give comes back to you – multiplied.

As Frederick William Robertson says, "You reap what you sow — not something else, but that. An act of love makes the soul more loving. A deed of humbleness deepens humbleness. The thing reaped is the very thing sown multiplied a hundredfold. You have sown a seed of life; you reap life everlasting."

The word "give" or its derivatives appear in the "self-help book," the Bible, over 1,729 times.

"I have found that among its other benefits, giving liberates the soul of the giver."
~ Maya Angelou

Philanthropy is not just something the rich have as a benefit. Philanthropy is not just the act of giving or donating money, it is also giving time, and service to benefit causes you care about the most. An act of a philanthropic nature promotes the common good and should improve human quality of life.

*"Love finds its most natural and spontaneous expression
in giving."*
~ Wallace Wattles

The Anonymous Giver
Giving really is the most selfish thing you can do. You get so much more out of it than its intended recipient does. One Christmas, Jeff and I decided to be a Secret Santa for a local family in need. We had decided on a particular budget of what we could afford. The process began, and something amazing happened. Although we set out to do only a certain amount of things for that family, we couldn't stop giving.

This was one of the most liberating experiences of our lives. We were supposed to just buy a toy for each child. However, by the time we were done, we had bought bicycles, sporting goods, clothes, etc. The best part was that the family did not know who we were. I should also preface this by saying that we had not yet shopped for our own children, nor did we have a lot of money at that time.

This kind of giving is different from buying a family member or friend a gift. If we are truly honest with ourselves, we often buy the gift hoping to really impress the person and to get a positive reaction from them. This is not the kind of giving I'm talking about here. We did not know these people and they did not know us. We did not have the restrictions of deciding whether they deserved it or not because last year they did not give us something or because we hadn't spoken in weeks.

We would never see the smiles on their faces or the tears of joy they would display while opening these gifts. It was a purely personal act of giving, without the benefit of the recipient's involvement. This proves that giving is selfish and very personal. We got back far more than we gave to that family in joy and thanksgiving. The feeling is something that cannot be explained; you must experience it for yourself. Before then, I never understood why there were anonymous givers, but now I do.

The Book of Matthew, Chapter 6, Verses 1-4 speaks of this very thing: *"Watch out! Don't do your good deeds publicly, to be admired by others, for you will lose the reward from your Father in heaven. When you give to someone in*

need, don't do as the hypocrites do – blowing trumpets in the synagogues and streets to call attention to their acts of charity! I tell you the truth, they have received all the reward they will ever get. But when you give to someone in need, don't let your left hand know what your right hand is doing. Give your gifts in private, and your Father, who sees everything, will reward you."

Often I have done things for people who will never know it. This way, I don't have to worry about them feeling the need to express gratitude when they would rather not – thus saving myself from the hurt and disappointment caused by ingratitude. I'm not suggesting that you always give anonymously; I am simply trying to prove that the recipient has nothing to do with the act. I was surprised to find that some people resent your ability to give and even question your intentions.

So by giving anonymously, it takes away the uncomfortableness from the recipient of having to show gratitude. While it is important to give, it is equally as important to learn how to receive. Lots of people are missing out on this reciprocal relationship because they are not good receivers.

> *"The love we give away is the only love we keep."*
> ~ Elbert Hubbard

Be a True Hero

Give inspiration and you will get inspired. Wayne Dyer said that inspiration is our ultimate calling, and I agree. Everywhere you look there are people who can inspire you. If you're looking to get inspired, try being an inspiration to someone else. In the act of doing so, you are elevated to a higher level and will discover newfound motivation for yourself.

You don't have to look for an answer to people's problems; you are the answer to someone's problems. So you may be thinking, "Yeah, but what about me? I'm looking for answers to my own problems. When I get it straight, I will inspire others." No, my friend, it doesn't quite work like that. You must first give before you can get, in that order.

In today's culture, we get caught up in what makes people great.

Our definition of greatness is twisted and distorted now. We are celebrity obsessed and we act as if a singer, actor or athlete is a hero because they can throw a ball far, run fast, sing high notes, or pretend to be someone else on our big screens. But does that make them great? Does that make them a hero? No. Each and every one of us can be a hero to someone. Each one of us can be great.

Greatness is not measured by what you have done but rather by what you have inspired others to do. If simply by virtue of you living your life maximized, you have inspired others to do the same, then you, my friend, are great.

"For life makes not mistakes and always gives man
that which man first gives himself."
~ Neville Goddard

You Will Reap What You Sow
You may not reap where you sow, but you will most assuredly reap what you sow. There are times when you are enthusiastically giving and helping someone in need. It may be a friend or a stranger. You may believe it is there, from those people, that you should reap your reward. That is not usually the case. You will be rewarded by giving. However, it may not come from the people you have directly helped.

A farmer may plant seeds in one area and reap his harvest in another. However that farmer, if he plants apple seeds, does not get oranges. He will confidently garner the benefits of exactly what he planted.

Another important thing to note is you must plant seeds in fertile soil. Your seeds have the capacity to grow and develop when planted in the rich, healthy soil. Your benevolence must be well thought out and planned. It is not wise to throw seeds around with reckless abandon. Be mindful what and where you are sowing.

Give respect, mercy, sensitivity, attention, time, grace, unmerited favor, etc., if that is what you require. If it is time you need, give time. If it is love you need, give love.

"One man gives freely, yet gains even more;
Another withholds unduly but comes to poverty.
A generous man will prosper; he who refreshes
Others will himself be refreshed."
~ Proverbs 11:24-25

"Tis Better to Give than Receive" – The Scientific Proof

The National Institute of Neurological Disorders and Stroke (NINDS), a division of the National Institute of Health (NIH), did research which revealed that when you give from the heart it actually satisfies the brain. They did a sort of brain imaging research by putting the subject through a series of activities. These activities modeled the acts of giving and receiving cash. They watched for brain activity and found some astonishing results. It turns out that the same regions of the brain that were associated with the good feelings and rewards of receiving things like cash were the same regions of the brain used when giving cash to charities and such. Also, other regions of the brain that were activated when giving were not activated when receiving.

They even went further in the study to suggest that we actually get more pleasure in the giving than in the receiving.

The best part of this study for me was that these subjects gave not because they were motivated by some expectation of received recognition or thanks. The brain activation occurred simply with the act of donation.

The act of giving produces just as much joy as the act of receiving, and in my opinion, giving actually produces more joy than receiving. The more we give, the more we put ourselves in a position to receive. But there is really a twist to this giving thing. Most people, when they think about giving, they think only of giving their money.

But the greatest gift you can give is the gift of yourself, your substance, your essence, your truth, your love. As you give, you will increase your own capacity to receive for one should be equal to the other. The one who receives more than he gives cannot be content, and the one who gives more than he receives cannot be fulfilled. We must give and receive in equal measure. Therefore, the more you give, the more you receive.

Selfishness Is Not Rewarded

I have often had a desire to give to others, and yet they were not in a position to receive. How can someone not be in a position to receive? Because they have not set themselves up to receive by giving of themselves in what capacity they could. Selfishness cannot be honored with the gift of receiving. Even if you tried to give of yourself or your substance to a selfish person, they would be unable to receive it, peacefully or joyfully, because they have not given of themselves or their substance.

The more you give of yourself to the world, the greater benefit you are to humankind, and as a byproduct, you are in the best position to receive all that the world has for you. If you want to receive... give. It's that simple.

Pay Any Price to Stay in the Company of Extraordinary People

"You must pay the price if you wish to secure the blessing."
~ Andrew Jackson

If it is your desire to have a successful journey full of joy, you must spend as much time as you can with extraordinary people. It is often said that we earn about as much as the five people we spend the most time with. So, if you have aspirations of having a happy marriage, hang with happily married people. If you aspire to have a successful business, spend time in the company of successful business people.

While I have had the pleasure of meeting some of the world's most fascinating people, my favorites were the people who achieved greatness in their life's work through a relentless pursuit of excellence. I've met Rosa Parks, Michelle Obama, Ruby Dee, Oprah Winfrey, Dr. Wayne Dyer, along with some of the greatest singers, actors, artists and authors on the planet, and I have greatly admired the work they've done for the world. There is actually nothing more beautiful for me to see than someone who loves what they do.

Passion Is Contagious

In any endeavor, there's nothing more attractive, and even sexy, than to watch someone do what they love to do. I love to spend time around people who are passionate about life. It's inspiring. I quickly learned that to be extraordinary, it requires you to be outside of the ordinary. Often these people are shunned until they do something that everyone recognizes as great.

But I love the misfits, the folks who marched to their own drum.

Somehow I knew those people heard something different, and I heard it too.

We once had a brother team of landscape architects who were working on a landscape design for the yard at our house. These guys were so passionate about dirt. They had me smelling different types of dirt to determine a certain quality of the soil. They drove me around to show me work that they had created around the neighborhood. These guys were as proud of their masterpieces as any adoring parent would be of their own children. I had never seen such passion about dirt. I loved being around those guys. They were extraordinary people who caused me to want to be better at what I did.

As a lover of food, any chef that cooks for me must be passionate about cooking. I don't want to eat the food of someone who is just cooking until their singing career takes off. No, no. That's not inspiring to me. I need to know that you love to cook, and if given the opportunity, you would do nothing else but that. I can go to a restaurant and eat a meal and just from the taste of that meal I can tell you if that Chef loves what they do or not. If you cook for me, your love of food should be evident.

Each time I eat a great meal, I am inspired to go home and attempt to duplicate that dish in my own kitchen because that passionate Chef inspired me to raise my cooking game a little higher.

My Extraordinary Friend – Pedro Santana
Along my journey, I have been blessed to have managed or been involved in the careers of artists who were extraordinary at what they did. Through that calling, I've had the opportunity of spending quite a bit of time with special people like the extraordinary Pedro Santana. Pedro was one of my favorite people. I was inspired every time I was around him. Pedro was a beautiful man. Puerto Rican born, he often dressed like a hippie. Wearing his naturally curly hair long was always my favorite look for him. I would always tell him he would be a shoo-in for the role of Jesus in a play or movie. No wigs or make-up necessary.

Santana's personality was much larger than his small frame could bear. While you wouldn't know it from looking at him, Pedro was a famed school Principal from the South Bronx. He profoundly and

220

positively impacted the lives of hundreds if not thousands of students over his short lifetime.

I know he surely impacted my life as I was just a witness to his. Pedro's students adored him because he was like them. Pedro used to call himself a special-ed student who was still learning in his own unique way. He had a way of reaching children that was so sweet and special; it was like poetry in motion when watching him at work.

Pedro lived his life on his own terms and transitioned in that same fashion. He is the first person that I know to plan his own funeral and make it a red carpet event.

Pedro was my friend. While he was always surrounded by adoring fans, friends, and family, whenever you were with him, he made you feel like it was just the two of you in the room. A talented performer, a brilliant educator, a dad, a husband, a brother, a son and a friend, Pedro Santana was an extraordinary person.

Connecting with Extraordinary People

If you can't seem to find extraordinary people, although they are surrounding all of us all the time, you must go and find them wherever you can. One of my favorite places to spend time is inside of a bookstore. It is there that I can surround myself with the thoughts, wisdom and advice of extraordinary people, dead or alive, without ever having to actually meet those people.

Through the books and teachings of Neville Goddard, Christian Larson, Wallace Wattles, and Napoleon Hill, most of which had passed away long before I was born, I am charged to be more by them. In these ways, I get to be mentored by these extraordinary people. These people and others have helped shape my B.S.

Today, with the Internet, you can connect with just about anyone and gain from their wisdom for next to nothing. But if you're given the opportunity to attend seminars, workshops and other events hosted by today's thought leaders, spare no expense and get there. No matter what the cost, the value to your life is far greater than the cost of admission.

Every chance I get, I attend the conferences of those who I wish to be taught and inspired by no matter where it is held in the country.

While these people have inspired me, most would not know their names. You won't find them on a billboard or a marquee. However, because of the unique approach they take to life, I am lifted higher, and I would do anything to stay in the company of those wonderful people.

You might consider establishing a mastermind group of people in your local area who are of like minds. Be sure that they are optimistic, motivated people who can bring something unique and special to your group. Meet with them on a regular basis and share your ideas and strategies. It's a powerful thing when people can get together from all walks of life to uplift and encourage each other to accomplish their goals and dreams. If it gets tough, don't worry, you are making what I like to call power moves. And if power moves were easy, everyone would be making them, but they're not.

"It has long since come to my attention that people of accomplishment rarely sat back and let things happen to them.
They went out and happened to things."
~ Leonardo Da Vinci

Learning from the Extraordinary
When I started The Shelley Roxanne Show, I wanted to meet extraordinary people, and I also wanted to introduce them to my listening audience. I appreciated the value of studying greatness. On my show, I've had the pleasure of hosting extraordinary people like Uncle Wally "Famous Amos," Joe Vitale, Lisa Nichols and other teachers from The Secret, Tim Wise, Steven Silbiger and so many more. I almost interviewed Steve Jobs.

His office, in fact, returned my producer's call and said that if Steve were ever to do interviews, which he did not regularly do, my show would be the one he would do. I was so honored to be even considered by Steve Jobs and that he could have possibly known who I was. There are extraordinary people that I would pay anything to be around. Steve Jobs would have been one of those people.

There is one thing that I understand all too well, and that is – You are constantly becoming. Either you are becoming like the people you are around, or they are becoming like you. Therefore, it pays to stay in

the company of people who are extraordinary. Spare no expense when it comes to improving yourself – mind, body, and spirit. While you should never copy anyone, you can be inspired by them.

Make a study of what makes the great great in your particular area of interest or endeavor. You can learn a lot by simply studying how someone else accomplished great things. Borrow ideas and strategies but put your own unique spin on it. There are patterns and commonalities among the people who have achieved great things. Success always leaves clues.

HELP Is Not a Four Letter Word

"It's as if we've divided the world into 'those who offer help' and 'those who need help.' The truth is that we are both.'
~ Brené Brown

This particular secret was a really big lesson for me. While I'm much better than I was with this one, I am still a work in progress. That is the fun of the journey, I suppose. It took a recent conversation with my wise son Evan to really break down the issue of asking for help.

Why is it so hard for us to do? After much research, I discovered the answer. The answer in one word is ego. That dreaded monster we have heard about all our lives. We have such a challenge asking for help because we don't want to appear that we need the help, but we do. How counterintuitive is that? On the one hand, we need something but we don't want to appear "needy". What a dilemma!

Ask & Don't Assume People Know

As a Virgo, who is used to being independent and self-sufficient, asking for help was the last thing that I ever wanted to do. But recently that is exactly what I had to do. Were it not for a few wonderful, loving people in my life, I would not have been able to get this book done and out into your hands. I would also not have been able to write this chapter. If I hadn't lived it, I wouldn't have been able to suggest that you live it too!

I was surprised, and humbled, to find that that there are people sitting around us just waiting to help us – but we must ask for the help. How else can they know you need it except that you put that evil monster of ego aside and ask them for assistance?

Even Jesus, who is all knowing, made the people express what it was that they wanted from him, even when it may have appeared obvious. When he asked the blind man, "What can I do for you?" surely that blind man must have thought, "Dude, can't you see I'm blind? Isn't it obvious what I want from you?" The truth is that it's not necessarily obvious to the people around us. We have to express with our words what it is that we want and need from them.

I heard a joke about a traveling evangelist who saw a man begging on the side of the road. The man was in a wheelchair and could not walk. The evangelist, without saying a word, ran over to the man, laid hands upon him, and healed the man instantly. The man was furious. He said to the evangelist, "What did you do that for? Now, what am I going to do to make money?" You see, the evangelist assumed that the man wanted to be healed, but he didn't. The healing cramped his lifestyle.

We can't expect people to assume we want help because it appears obvious. Also, there are times when their help is not in our best interests and will stunt our own growth and progress. (I discussed this in the "Break the Shell" chapter.) The challenge here is us learning how to ask for help and being OK with the answer – whatever that is.

Fear of a "No" Answer
Somehow I was under the misconception that if I asked you for help, then that made me weak. But what I learned is that it demonstrates my strength. No one can get through this journey alone. You need help from others and the quicker you ask for it, the sooner you'll get it.

Don't worry; help is not a four letter word. First, what are we really afraid of? I first thought that I was afraid of someone saying no if I asked for help, and to me that was partly my problem.

I had a serious issue with being disappointed by people I care about, so I didn't want to give them the opportunity to disappoint me. I work so hard not to disappoint others because I loathe being disappointed myself. I suppose I felt that if I asked you for help, and you were in a position to help me, and you said no, that it would change our relationship. To be honest, completely honest, it probably would. And I didn't want that, so I didn't ask. I'd rather believe that if you were in a position to, you would help me. So I didn't take any chances.

What I've learned is that no is just another answer. If you ask for something and the person says no, that's fine. You didn't have it before and so nothing changes.

Digging Deeper

I don't really think it was the no itself that bothered me the most; it was something more than that. Somehow I got the impression that it said something about me that I would even need to ask.

For years and years, I just wouldn't ask for help. Therefore, I was overwhelmed and overburdened much of the journey. It was only if someone volunteered the help that I would accept it, and even then, it was not easy. I marveled at how other people could come to me, time and time again, and ask me to help them with no hesitation or fear. I wanted that kind of freedom.

So I did the introspection work to figure out what makes it easy for some people to ask for help and not for others, like me. As usual, the answer is always right in front of us hidden in plain sight; the culprit, as I stated at the beginning of the chapter, was none other than ego. Ego convinces you that you don't need anyone's help and that you and you alone can do whatever you need to be done in your life. It convinces you that you will appear weak and needy to the person you're asking for the help. Don't fall for it, like I did. It's a deception.

EGO – Edging God Out

So what, or who is ego? I'm sure that as you read this, there are spiritual workshops, seminars and gatherings happening all around the world with awakened conscious seekers looking to slay that thing they call the ego. I'm not sure all of that is necessary. I personally see it much simpler than that. Ego is simply that part of us that is unsure and unaware of our greatness. Ego is our self-image protector. Like a bodyguard for the self-image. But that bodyguard often goes rogue and gets out of control.

Wayne Dyer brilliantly said ego stands for Edging God Out. I agree wholeheartedly with Dr. Dyer. Imagine your life as a continuum. At one end of the line is Ego, the insecure part of you, and at the other end is God, the complete and wholeness of you. The further you travel towards

ego, the further away from God you move, and vice versa. Where we live on that continuum determines the quality of our journey.

The closer you are to your whole, complete awesomeness, the slower you are to take offense to things. Meanwhile, your ego causes you to make decisions that may not be in your own best interest but are in the best interest of ego. But ego offers you nothing good. Ego is insatiable, unreasonable and often dangerous. While some psychologists may suggest that a healthy ego is important, I think it is an oxymoron. How can insecurity ever be healthy?

Blind to the Benefits

Not long ago, I had what started out to be a casual conversation with a physician. She was telling me about how open-minded she is about the things of the world and how she loved to help people and so on. The conversation began to take a weird turn for the worse when she began to talk about her experience of trying to get into a particular internship program at a prestigious hospital. She told me about how the director of the hospital intentionally put roadblocks in her way to stop her from getting into the program. She lamented about how she had to do hours of extra work to be even considered.

While she told me that she did eventually get into the program, she would never ever forgive the man who wasted her time in his effort to stop her from getting in. I suggested to her that she consider that the experience was designed for her good, but she didn't have it. She felt that this guy didn't like her, and he was just evil and wanted to stop her from being part of the program.

She said his behavior was unforgivable because he "took her time" away from her. What started out as a casual conversation between us turned ugly as she was offended by my suggestion that the experience was good for her. After all, she did eventually get what she wanted – she got into the program in spite of the director's efforts. I say it was ugly because her ego seemed to take over her as if she were possessed by an alien. It became all about what he did to her, the time he took from her, the extra work he caused her to have to do, blah, blah, blah. This beautiful woman became possessed by something ugly right before my

eyes and at that point there was no going back for us.

It's a rare occasion when I lose an argument (that's my ego talking) but that time her ego won. We did hug it out in the end, but her ego didn't back down. Sadly she missed, due to her ego, the entire point. The experience she had in getting into that internship program strengthened her. She learned resolve; she found determination she didn't know she had, and she achieved a lifelong goal. The situation was designed to make her better, but all she ended up becoming was bitter. That's what ego does to us. It puts a blinder on us and doesn't allow us to see clearly the situation for what it truly is.

A Tough Challenge
I'm not sure that we can ever completely get rid of ego. Perhaps that will be when we're walking in our full God-ness. Until then, it's surely something that I work to keep in check. HELP!

PART SEVEN

SUCCESS
TOOLS

Dare Something Worthy

"In any moment of decision, the best thing you can do is the right thing. The worst thing you can do is nothing."
~ Theodore Roosevelt

If there were ever a time to dare, to make a difference, to embark on something worth doing, it is now. Not for any grand cause necessarily, but for something that tugs at your heart, something that's your aspiration or dream.

Inspired by My Mother, Glo

That's what happened to me in 2007. It was shortly after my mother, Glo, had transitioned. I was inspired by the amount of people my mother impacted with her life. She wasn't a TV star or a radio personality or even a politician, yet she changed people's lives in a major way. Not just a few, she impacted thousands. Glo's funeral was such an event that the entire town was virtually shut down due to the traffic of people who came from far and wide to pay their last respects to this remarkable woman. It's believed that there were over 5,000 people in attendance that day.

There are trees planted in Israel in her name, and she was not even Israeli or Jewish. She has monuments and scholarships that bear her name and likeness. She was a simple woman with a huge heart. Glo loved people, and they loved her right back. She had a special place for the misfits. I used to call her the friend of the friendless.

It was always Glo's dream to start an organization for children. She was definitely the "kid whisperer." Children loved Glo. She related to them in a way that no other adult could. It's as if their spirits were aligned. Although Glo did not live, in the physical sense, to see her dream

233

realized, I was inspired to start an organization of my own for children. And that's how Optimistic Leadership Academy for Boys (OLAB) was born.

Helping Boys/Young Men
OLAB is an initiative that I founded to support the care and development of young men. As a mother of three sons, I have a heart for boys. I hear them, I feel for them, and I was deeply concerned about what I saw in society. Too many of our boys and young men were falling behind in school and life. They were under motivated and performing well below expectations - especially compared to the girls their age.

Boys receive the majority of the Ds and Fs given to all students, and they create 90% of classroom discipline problems. In elementary school, boys are two times more likely than girls to be diagnosed with learning disabilities and twice as likely to be placed in special education classes.

While these statistics may have been facts, for me it was not the truth. These stats were both staggering and unacceptable. I sought to get to the root of this problem. OLAB was created to take these important issues head-on. I sought to find optimistic solutions to what appeared to be a complex problem and thus OLAB was born. My vision for the Academy was to help the boy find the hero within himself and to inspire the excellence in him to shine through.

At OLAB, we give our boys the understanding that their lives are comprised of their choices, and we are sure, with the right tools, they will choose to succeed.

Turn Your Mess into Your Message
Life can get messy but don't worry, your mess eventually becomes your message. Notice that often the champions for a cause have either personally experienced what they're trying to change or someone they love has. It's the mothers who have lost children due to drunk driving that began M.A.D.D. (Mothers against Drunk Driving). This wonderful organization has made major strides in bringing attention to underage drinking and drunk driving. We have all benefited from their message. It's those who suffered from cancer that have made strides in cancer

research.

It's parents whose children are afflicted with autism who are bringing the world's attention to this disorder. Alcoholics Anonymous, an organization that has helped millions stop drinking, would not be in existence were it not for those who experienced alcoholism and then freed themselves through the process of gaining back sobriety. The only way for them to free others was for them first to free themselves. Their mess became their message.

I have attended many AA events in celebration of the sobriety of others. I'm most impressed by one of the prayers used by AA during the Twelve Step process, often referred to as the Sobriety-Prayer or Serenity Prayer. When you have gone through things, you are the person who is best equipped to help others who are going through that same thing. While you develop from the negatives, it's not for you alone. It is for a greater good.

We Are All Messengers

You may not travel the world, as some do, spreading your message; rather it may be your family alone that benefits from your efforts. Perhaps there is something that has plagued your family for generations, and it is incumbent upon you to end that generational curse. Instead of accepting it as your fate, because your father had it and his father had it, do something about it to stop the cycle. You and generations after you will benefit from it. It's sort of like turning lemons into lemon meringue pie. Who doesn't love lemon meringue pie?

Become an expert in getting yourself better and then you can help others. Often, things happen simultaneously. As you take the focus off of your problems and focus on a solution, it impacts far more than you. It is written, when you refresh others, you yourself will be refreshed.

Go Big or Go Bigger

"When your heart is in your dreams,
no request is too extreme."
~ Jiminy Cricket

Throughout my career as an entrepreneur, there were many times when we sat before investors and venture capitalists. Each time, the first question they ask you is "How much money do you need to accomplish your goals?" That may not seem unusual to you but what comes next surprises me still. It seems the bigger the amount, the more interested they become in your project. This means all those times that you ask for $25,000, $50,000 or $100,000; you are not taken seriously because the bigger the dream, the better.

If these people are going to invest in your project, they want to be assured that you are a big thinker. Investors want a big return on investment and, therefore, the bigger the investment, the bigger the return. This philosophy many not sound practical to you who think, "Well, the less I borrow, the less I have to pay back." That may be true, but the investor thinks that you'll eventually run out of money, and the project could be in jeopardy of failing – which means they lose their money.

For them, that is a big red flag. I'm not suggesting that you ask for money you do not need. I am however suggesting that you be sure you have enough capital to ensure the success of your project in the long term. Don't limit yourself because you're guilty of thinking too small.

Living Large
Many of the people who know me well often tease me about the fact

that I don't ever do anything small. They tease me about my jewelry, my house, my car and my husband – all considered by some to be rather large for their given categories. Perhaps I should have been born in Texas since I hear they like to do everything big there in the Lone Star State.

I once met a woman who told me she could never wear a diamond as large as five karats. Her reasoning? She didn't want to walk around with the fear that someone would attack her for her ring. Is she serious? Surely she did not think I bought that nonsense? If the man of her dreams presented her with a beautiful sparkling diamond ring of five karats, I doubt she would turn it away because she was afraid of getting attacked.

But I do buy the fact that she would rather discount the desire for such a large ring and even justify the downsides of having it because she has not asked for one. Not everyone wants a large diamond ring, but I did and do, and I was willing to ask for it. When Jeff and I were dating, and he asked me what size ring I wore, I confidently answered, "Three karats or more." After he had caught his breath, Jeff learned that he was marrying someone who was learning how to ask for what she wanted, and her wants were big. Better he find out early than later, right?

"God gives us dreams a size too big so that we can grow in them. Dream BIG."
~ Angela Brook

Honor God with Big Dreams
Don't try to shrink your dreams to fit what you "think" is possible. Raise your standards. Be unreasonable. Often God will not meet your desires because they are too small for you.

Have you ever tried to purchase a pair of shoes that were too small for your feet? The very thought of walking in shoes two sizes too small for me makes me cringe right now. But that's what we do with our goals and dreams. We set goals that we think are reasonable or attainable, and we go for those. Very often, it's a goal that is not very broad or vast, has no complexity or range, but we think it is "realistic" so we go for it. That is the worst thing you can ever do. You must dream big. God is honored when our dreams and goals are bodacious, and we bring them to him in faith. He is faithful to give us what we desire. The bigger, the better.

God is big. We should never ask him to come down to our size; we should reach up to his. Although Jesus did great works in his time on earth, he told us that we would do greater works than he did. Jesus healed the sick, raised the dead, made the lame walk, and even turned water into wine at a wedding. It is written, we have those same abilities but only greater.

God Delivers Requests in His Name

It's also written that whatever we ask in God's name, that will He do. "Whatever" is a huge range. It leaves nothing out. It makes no conditions. Nowhere does it say, "Whatever you ask, as long as it is reasonable, I will do it. It says whatever." As far as I'm concerned, that means no limits need be put on anything I can ask for as long as it is in His name. That is the only condition. Is that too hard? I think not.

This is the confidence we have in approaching God; that if we ask anything according to His will, He hears us. And if we know that He hears us in whatever we ask, we know that we have the requests that we have asked from Him. I think that is awesome. You're probably thinking, "So let me get this right. You mean to tell me that whatever I ask of God, no matter how big, as long as I ask it according to His will, He hears me? And then as long as I'm willing to believe that He hears me, I can know for sure that I have the petitions/requests I have asked for? Wow, that's is a good deal." Yes, my friend, it is, and it is too good, and it is true. (See 1 John 5:14-15.)

Remember, while I encourage you to believe in who and what you want. These are the benefits to being a believer in Jesus. You can ask whatever you wish, and it will be done for you. (John 15:7). That is a guarantee. Where else can you get such a deal?

Stretch Yourself

There's nothing like a dream to create the future. Dream big, set ambitious goals, and truly believe in endless possibilities. Hold on to the dreams of your youth for you can win if you don't quit. Set goals beyond your reach but within your grasp. The stretch will be well worth it.

Your life is an occasion; rise to it.

Those Who Tell You Money Is the Root of All Evil Don't Have Any

"Wisdom is more precious than money,
and nothing compares to her."
~ Proverbs 8:11

I would be remiss if I didn't discuss the phenomenon called money. It's a great source of frustration for a believer. This is critical for your journey that we cover this important topic. Thousands of books are written about it, so we don't need to go over what you're to do with it. I just want to discuss the concept itself and dispel some myths so you won't fall for the deception.

I've always been fascinated by what people are willing to do to get this thing called money. I'm amazed by the havoc money, or the lack thereof has caused. There are good and bad things attributed to money, mostly bad, and yet it seems to be the driving force in many people's lives. It's said that of the 32 parables in the Bible, 16 of them relate to money. So, let's face it, money matters.

Hot Interview with Robert Kiyosaki
I've had the distinct pleasure of interviewing Robert Kiyosaki on The Shelley Roxanne Show. What an experience that was! Robert Kiyosaki is the author and creator of The *Rich Dad Poor Dad* Empire. Robert's book *Rich Dad Poor Dad* is now regarded as the #1 best-selling personal finance book of all time. I love Robert. He is passionate and unapologetic about his views about money and financial freedom.

Through his books, games and other products and services, his company Rich Dad has helped millions of people change the way they think about money. The show I did with Robert was probably one of the most controversial, heated exchanges that we've ever had with my

listeners.

Many were taken aback, even offended, by Robert's strong views regarding wealth and how to obtain it. Robert's belief is that most of us were not taught the correct rules of money early in life, and, therefore, need to be re-taught. Robert said that growing up he was blessed with the opportunity to learn from his best friend's father, his Rich Dad, how to mitigate risk and maximize profit, and it's his goal to share that information with the world. However, he believes that most people were taught how to be broke from their "Poor Dads." Robert challenges our education system and believes that since everyone uses it, we should teach children about money in our schools as early as possible.

Robert Kiyosaki and I talked about the misconception that money is the root of all evil. People actually believe that it says so in the Bible. It begs clarification. First, money has no characteristic. It simply takes on the characteristic of the person who has it. The media is even doing its job to contribute to the misconception. In just about any movie, the bad guy is always rich, the good guy is always poor. Subconsciously it is doing a job on the psyche of our world. Subconsciously, people – while they want to have money – don't want to feel themselves to be a bad person for having it.

This dichotomy is causing such a problem in our society. We have all experienced what is often called "money problems." I realized, albeit quite late in life, that money wasn't the problem at all. The problem was the focus that was placed on it. We give money far too much power. We've got to mend our broken relationship with money. We need to kiss and make up with money.

Examining Your Relationship with Money
Money can do a lot of things, but mostly it gives you options. You don't really want the money. You want the options that money provides. The money alone, just sitting under your mattress or in your bank, can do nothing on its own. It's what you do with it. You give your money life.

To have the options, we must first examine our relationship with money. What do you think about money? Do you think money is bad? Do you believe people who have it are bad? If you do, you will not be able

242

to attract money. Money is nothing more than energy, which is attracted or repelled. By judging money as bad, you're subconsciously repelling it from you. My friend, I've got news for you. It is OK to have money.

It's actually necessary to have money, as long as money doesn't have you. This is what Timothy was talking about in 1 Timothy when he said that "For the love of money is the root of all kinds of evil." He goes on to say that "Some people, eager for money, have wandered from the faith and pierced themselves with many griefs." Popular rapper The Notorious B.I.G. even sings about money's downside in his tune, "Mo' Money, Mo' Problems."

Unfortunately, Timothy's often quoted scripture is many times taken out of context. Money is not the root of all evil or you wouldn't be working so hard for it. Instead, it's the obsession, the relentless pursuit of it, without regard for what is right and good, that's evil. Not the money itself.

Frankly, things cost money. Life's necessities cost money. Education costs. Studying to find cures for diseases cost money. Living the life you were destined to live costs money. As author Rita Davenport says, "Money isn't everything, but it's right up there with oxygen."

I've found that money is an amplifier. It simply makes you more of what you already are. If you're a good person, money will help you to be even better. If you're a bad, or an evil person, money will permit you to be even more evil. Money simply exposes you. But don't let it control you. This is where the problem comes in. The issue with money is that we have a dysfunctional relationship with it. Essentially we and money need to go through couple's therapy in order to get back together. Time to mend this broken relationship.

A Love/Hate Relationship
Money is simply a form of currency used to trade goods and services. At one time, money took the form of cattle, herds, livestock, silver, gold and more. Even today, money is represented by plastic or simply numbers on a page. Nowadays, you can buy things with your smartphone, computer or thumbprint without ever touching that physical thing we call "money." It appears that money is not really money; it's a concept.

Remember, it's not really the money you want, it's options that the concept offers you. But before you get the options, you must fix your love/hate relationship with money. On one hand, you love it but on another hand you hate what it represents. You're sending money mixed signals. You want to be seen with it in public but don't treat it properly or with respect in private. You lust after its benefits and yet you act in public like you don't really care about it when you actually do. Sounds to me like a relationship that needs healing. Maybe you should check your B.S. about money.

It's OK to Like Money

I would say yes, it's actually OK to like money. You can even love and appreciate it. The love of money only becomes a problem when you love it above everything else that is more important. But you must ask yourself whether you're already doing that. The fact is; you leave your family for it every day. You spend more time trying to get it than you do anything else.

Money is one of the biggest reasons for divorce because couples disagree about how to spend it, make it, and save it. So I think we have established that in order to free yourself from the frustration that may exist due to a perceived lack of money, it's important to examine your relationship with money. The sooner you're OK with money, money will be OK with you. You won't have to chase money because it won't be running away from you any longer. You'll be a money magnet.

Ask, Seek, Knock, Repeat

"Knock, And He'll open the door
vanish, and He'll make you shine like the sun
fall, and He'll raise you to the heavens
become nothing, and He'll turn you into everything."
~ Rumi

Know that whatever you want and need for your journey, as long as you are persistent in asking, you will receive. It's written that, if you ask and keep on asking, it shall be given you; seek and keep on seeking and you shall find; knock and keep on knocking and the door shall be opened to you. For everyone who asks and keeps on asking receives; and he who seeks and keeps on seeking finds; and to him who knocks and keeps on knocking, the door shall be opened.

There's an Art to Asking

I am always astounded by people's inability to ask for things they desire. You may not realize that 95% of the things you have now are because you asked for them. If you don't ask, however, you'll be guaranteed not to get what you want 100% of the time. You must be persistent.

Children are great at asking for what they want. The younger, the better. Young children have not learned that rejection simply means you haven't provided enough information to the person you want something from. Don't be afraid of a "No". No is just another answer. However, you will not get what you really want unless you ask for it and are specific. Specificity eliminates confusion and error.

Imagine going to a restaurant. The waitress approaches your table and greets you. You are fully aware that she's there to take your order. What do you think would happen if you just sat there staring at her? She is there to take your order; you and she are both fully aware of that fact.

You are also aware that if you don't ask for what you want, you surely will not get it. Furthermore, you're definitely not going to get exactly what you want if you're not specific. If you tell her to just bring you some food, you are likely to get something you don't like. If you're ordering a steak, most servers will ask you more qualifying questions to prevent you from getting something unacceptable to you. They will often ask you, "How do you want that steak?"

You then are perhaps more specific by telling them you want your steak rare, medium, medium well, etc. If you didn't ask for something to drink with your order, you wouldn't get it. If you wanted an appetizer but didn't ask for it, you wouldn't be served an appetizer. The same thing goes for the Universe. You have not the things you desire because you have not asked for them, and/or you have not been specific enough about the details.

*"The indispensable first step to getting the
things you want out of life is this: decide what you want."*
~ Ben Stein

Asking the Right Questions
There are few things I have asked for that I have not received. But there are a lot of things I wanted but failed to ask for, and, therefore, I didn't get them. Many times you have not received, simply because you haven't asked the right questions.

Once Jeff and I had rented a beautiful condo on the beach. When we moved in, we were told by the realtor that the condo association no longer had a relationship with the beach club that they were previously using. Jeff and I were told, when we looked at the place, that they were in the process of searching for a new way to accommodate the residents. So, each time we went down to the beach, we schlepped our own chairs, towels, umbrellas, food and drink.

For the two years that we stayed there, we went through the painstaking inconvenience of brushing off the sand and cleaning off the stuff each time we went back up to the condo. If we were hungry and didn't bring our own food, we'd have to pack up and leave the beach in order to go and get something to eat. Eventually, it became so much of a chore that we went down to the beach less and less.

For two whole years, we complained to each other about the exorbitant amount of money that we were paying for the condo and how we felt that the condo association should have a beach club by now. But we never asked anyone about it. The conversation, and complaining, remained amongst the two of us. It was not until we were just about ready to move out that I happened to learn something I didn't know.

One of the last days there at the condo, I was headed down to the beach with our regular routine of chairs and umbrella in tow, and the concierge asked me if I needed a ride to the beach club. "What beach club?" I asked. He replied, "The Beach Club for our condo that we have had for the last two years." He said, "You can walk, or I can drive you there." In shock, I hopped into his van – marked Beach Club by the way – and he took me to a stunningly beautiful private beach club. It was gorgeous. It had a restaurant, store, pools, cabanas and towel service. They bring you umbrellas and set up cushy lounge chairs for you. A full-service beach club was available to us the entire time, but we didn't know it.

While we could blame the realtor for not advising us of this fact, it was not his fault. We should have asked the right questions, and we didn't. You cannot assume that people know what you want and need unless you are specific in your asking. It costs us time and money, not to mention missed fun, by not simply asking the right questions.

"Don't think of him as a seeker...
Whatever he's looking for, he is that himself."
~ Rumi

One Man Kept Asking
We can learn a lot from some of the world's best salespeople. They certainly know how to Ask, Seek, Knock, Repeat.

In 1980, a young man named Alfredo Bala walked into an open opportunity meeting for a Direct Sales Organization in Warwick, Rhode Island and the course of his life was forever changed. Al was excited about the opportunity to be in business for himself while at the same time helping others to achieve their dreams and goals as well.

With hard work, Al moved up the ranks. He dedicated his life to the service of others. He asked, sought, knocked, then asked and knocked some more. Al traveled the globe seeking people who he could help to create the lifestyle of their dreams. He didn't take "No" for an answer. He kept on knocking; he kept on seeking, he kept on asking.

Today, Al Bala is the inspirational leader, CEO and President of Mannatech, Incorporated. Mannatech develops high-quality health, weight, fitness, and skin care products that are based on the solid foundation of nutritional science and development standards. Al and his teams move their products around the world through a platform they call "Social Selling." Essentially, they teach people to ask, seek, knock, repeat.

35 years after walking into that meeting in Rhode Island, Al Bala is changing the world by fostering a culture of social entrepreneurship and wellness for millions of people around the globe.

"At first dreams seem impossible, then improbable, then inevitable."
- Christopher Reeve

Keep on Knocking
Finding is reserved for the seekers. You will only find if you are seeking. You've got to seek and keep seeking, knock and keep knocking. Eventually, doors will be opened to you.

Hugh "Peanuts" Whalum is the perfect expression of a knocker who kept on knocking. Peanuts Whalum is a pianist, singer, tenor saxophonist and outright musical genius who played with the likes of Ella Fitzgerald, Nat King Cole, Miles Davis and many more. After knocking for 62 years, Peanuts finally was signed to his first solo recording contract at the tender age of 73. He released his self-titled debut album in August 2006.

I interviewed Peanuts on The Shelley Roxanne Show after I saw him perform at a jazz festival on my birthday many years ago. Peanuts' performance that night was so inspiring on so many levels. I was left in tears of joy. I had never heard a voice as sweet and velvety smooth as his.

I had to know this man.

My talk with Peanuts was one of the highlights for me as he is one of the nicest, most charming men you'll ever meet.

Now at 80 years young, Peanuts Whalum will not be stopped. He performs regularly and is finally getting the recognition that he so deserves. Peanuts shines his light with unparalleled brightness, and, as a result, gives the rest of us permission to do the same. He finally has taken his rightful place among the greats, right where he belonged all along. Peanuts never gave up and neither should you.

Change the Game

If life is a game, we were put on this planet not just to play the game; we also are supposed to change the game. In your given area or life's work, you are to raise the bar. When you raise the bar, you change what you demand of yourself and everyone else around you.

Be a Tiger
We have seen people in history, distant and recent, who have changed the game. Tiger Woods has single-handedly changed the game of golf. Mark Zuckerberg has changed the game of how people communicate on the Internet. Steve Jobs has changed the game. Venus and Serena Williams have changed the game. Barack Obama has changed the game. Oprah Winfrey has changed the game. Martin Luther King changed the game. Mother Teresa changed the game. Thomas Edison changed the game. Rosa Parks changed the game. Michael Phelps changed the game. Larry Page and Sergey Brin changed the game. J.K. Rowling changed the game. Diana Nyad changed the game. I could go on, but you get the point. Each one of these people raised the bar in their particular area or life's work. You are capable – and responsible – to do the same.

Be a Thermostat
No matter what you were purposed to do, you've got to raise the bar. In your office, in your school, in your business, in your sport, in your family, you must strive to lift the bar up higher. Change the temperature.

Bring the heat. We were put on this planet to be thermostats and not thermometers. A thermometer reflects the temperature of the environment while thermostats control the temperature. I'm sure you know a lot of thermometers; those people who read and reflect the environment they are in.

These folks will complain about the environment but won't do anything about it. They are complacent, frustrated, downtrodden, lazy or simply believe that the way it is will always be that way. But then, every once in a while, here comes a thermostat. That person certainly recognizes the temperature and the environment, but they also recognize their responsibility to adjust and change it. They're willing to work, even when they have to take some heat. Thermostats can walk in a room and bring warmth to the coldest place. Are you a thermostat or a thermometer in your environment – be it at work, home or community? Can you take the heat and bring the heat when necessary?

Do what you do so well, that others have to come up to your standard just to compete. Game changers don't wait for opportunities to make a difference; they go out and create those opportunities. Game changes are risk-takers. If you're not living on the edge, you're taking up too much space. Be willing to go out on a limb because that is where the fruit is.

"If opportunity doesn't knock, build a door."
~ Milton Berle

Do It For The Outcome, Not the Income
Take what you have been given and increase its value. You're not paid for the time you give; you're paid for the value you offer. Work to increase your value in the marketplace and you will increase your income. Never settle for good when great is possible. Do the work you were called to do, not for the income, do it for the outcome. John F. Kennedy was quoted as saying, "Never accept second place when first is available." Well, first place is always available; it's up to you to take it.

Steve Jobs, the creator of Apple Computers, was and still is an inspiration to me and of course to millions. If you or anyone close to you

uses any of his products, you can attest to his genius. But Steve clearly was a misfit and often misunderstood, with reason. The guy didn't like to wear shoes; he didn't like to follow rules, and he danced to the beat of his own drum. Steve couldn't waste his time worrying about what you thought of him. He was too busy changing the world – your world.

It's because of Steve that today I sit and type these words on a computer that can fit in my purse with my lipstick and my keys. Steve Jobs changed the game, and I'm thankful for that. Where would we all be if Steve allowed himself to turn down the intensity of who he was and what he could create simply to please those around him? Dr. Seuss said it best: "Be who you are and say what you feel because those who mind don't matter and those who matter don't mind."

It is written that we are to have dominion. Dominion means to dominate. We are not to accept mediocrity in any area of our lives. Don't make any excuses for not bringing your "A" game to your life's work or profession. Each one of the people I highlight in this chapter had a valid excuse for not changing the game. But they did it anyway.

You may not have been born with the right pedigree or have enough money or even think you have enough talent. All those things are reasons but not excuses. Do it anyway. Life is full of risks. That is the truth. Low-risk living is a sin. Anyone who tells you that you have nothing to lose is lying. You can always lose something, but that's the beauty of it. Anything that is not worth losing is not worth having.

Crazy Ones Change the Game
Rob Siltanen and copywriter Ken Segall wrote a brilliant add for Apple back in 1997 for their Think Different Campaign. The ad was written to essentially announce to the world that Steve Jobs had returned to Apple after his departure in 1985. It is said that the commercial with Jobs narrating went viral after his transition in 2011. It stands alone as one of my favorite quotes. Perhaps because I identify so much with its message. It reads.

"Here's to the crazy ones, the misfits, the rebels, the troublemakers, the round pegs in the square holes... the ones who see things differently -- they're not fond of rules... You can quote them, disagree with them, glorify or vilify them, but the only thing you can't do is ignore them because they change things... they push the human race forward, and while some may see them as the crazy ones, we see genius, because the ones who are crazy enough to think that they can change the world, are the ones who do."
- Steve Jobs, Inventor (1955-2011)

Some Will, Some Won't, So What!

"It isn't that you have to smile at everything.
It is to accept the hard times like the great ones."
~ Sheila Pons

Oprah Winfrey is arguably the most famous person in the world, or at least she has been one of the most influential people in the world. And that is because of the incredible work she has done as an iconic TV presence. Oprah has been part of our lives for the last 30 years on television. But before we knew who Oprah Winfrey was, Oprah knew who she was. Long before Oprah Winfrey was a household name, young Oprah was fired from her job and told she was "unfit" for television news. Oprah's attitude was so what... somewhere, someone will see exactly who and what I am and I won't stop until I find them.

She had that same attitude many years later when she auditioned and landed the part of Sofia in The Color Purple movie. This was after her syndicated show had begun but long before she was an international sensation. When Steven Spielberg, the movie's director, was preparing the movie poster for the marketing of the film, Oprah asked Steven if he was going to put her name on the poster. Steven was bewildered as to why she would think that he would put a virtual unknown on the movie's poster. Steven told her, "Rae Dawn Chong is a star, you're not." Oprah answered Steven and said, "Someday everyone will know my name." Steven shrugged it off and told her, "Well, this is now, and we're not putting your name on the poster."

Fast forward ahead to 2010 when the film's cast was celebrating its 25th anniversary. As a nod to Oprah, Quincy Jones, one of the producers, had the film's poster remade placing Oprah's name on it, and he sent it to

Oprah as a gift. Now that she had become that household name, and the person who every brand would do anything to persuade her to endorse them – just like Oprah knew she would be – she went back to Steven Spielberg and said, "You see, Steven, you should've put my name on that poster."

Let Go & Keep Moving Forward
We call him the great innovator – animation entrepreneur Walt Disney – but at one point, Mr. Disney was told by a newspaper editor who was firing Walt that he was "not creative enough." Walt was told by the editor of the Kansas City Star that he "lacked imagination and had no good ideas." And to that Walt said, Some will, some won't, so what! Can you imagine that the man who later went on to create Mickey Mouse and the happiest place on Earth was once told he lacked imagination? It's ludicrous, right?

Well, it is now, but perhaps back then the editor felt justified in his assessment of Walt's talent (or lack thereof). Perhaps now someone is telling you that you lack what it takes to be great in your field of choice. No matter, don't give up! At some point, that person may end up working for you or at least reading about you in Fortune magazine in an article describing you as one of the richest people in the world.

> *"Do what you feel in your heart to be right,*
> *for you'll be criticized anyway."*
> ~ Eleanor Roosevelt

Michael Bloomberg is one of the richest men on the planet, and he got that way by using his severance money to start his own business after being let go from his position at investment house Salomon Brothers. Michael Bloomberg also said some will, some won't, so what!

Success through Persistence
Harland Sanders, after experiencing both success and failure in life and business, found himself broke and alone at the age of 65. He was a failure who had gotten fired from a dozen jobs before starting his restaurant.

Then he failed at that when he went out of business and found himself broke again. Instead of being bitter about his situation, he changed the way he looked at his problem. Harland took an inventory of what he had "in his hand." He realized that he had an awesome recipe for chicken that people really liked. He also had a $105 Social Security check.

He drove around in his Cadillac for two whole years, sleeping in his car, begging diner owners to buy and use his chicken recipe. He was asking for only a nickel for each chicken. Colonel (Harland) Sanders heard the word "no" over a thousand times before getting one "yes." It took him two years of asking, seeking and knocking before the door was opened to him. Would you do that? Do you believe in what you're doing enough to be rejected over a thousand times for two years before getting one "yes"? The 65-year-old Colonel did, and that's why we have finger lickin' good fried chicken today.

> *"There's no reason to be the richest man in the cemetery.*
> *You can't do any business from there."*
> ~ Colonel Harland Sanders

Bill Gates has said that everything is a good idea once it becomes a good idea. He actually has been quoted as saying that an idea is not good until everyone else thinks you're crazy to do it. Sounds like Bill might be on to something. I know for me, I would still be sitting around waiting for people to think the things I did were good ideas if I needed that validation. Thank God, I didn't because you wouldn't be reading this book if I had.

Pitching SpongeBob SquarePants
I have always been amazed by the massive success of the phenomenon known as SpongeBob SquarePants. I can only imagine those conversations that Stephen Hillenburg, the creator, was having in his initial pitch meetings. I would imagine that the conversation went something like this…

<u>Stephen:</u> "I have an idea to create an animated character named SpongeBob. He is actually a sponge and lives under the sea. His

house will be a pineapple and his best friend will be a Starfish."
<u>Network Exec:</u> "Are you crazy? Get out of here and take your sponge and his squarepants with you. This will never work."
<u>Stephen:</u> "Oh well, some will, some won't, so what!"

Due to his willingness to believe in his vision no matter what – even when people thought his idea was dumb – Hillenburg has gone on to win an Emmy Award and six Annie Awards for SpongeBob SquarePants. He has also received other awards, such as Heal the Bay's Walk the Talk Award for his efforts on elevating marine life awareness through SpongeBob SquarePants, and the Television Animation Award from the National Cartoonists Society. Thanks to Stephen, SpongeBob is a loving member of many families, including mine.

Let Patience Do Her Thing

"Patience is bitter, but its fruit is sweet."
~ Aristotle

We are in the age of instant everything. Instant coffee, instant downloads, blah blah blah. When I grew up, on Thanksgiving Day, it took more than 8 hours to cook the turkey for our dinner. Mom would get up early in the morning to season it and put it in the oven so that we could eat by 4 or 5 p.m. that day. Today, I cook a turkey in 45 minutes.

But back in the day, you just had to wait for things. Today "ain't nobody got time for that." I even find myself pressing the button numerous times on the keyboard if something doesn't load quickly enough, as if seconds are too long to wait. If a pizza cannot be made, boxed and delivered before we even hang up the phone, we somehow want it free. What has happened to patience?

Technology Fuels Our Impatience

I'm still amazed how FedEx can get a package way across the country quicker than I can drive from Manhattan to Brooklyn in rush hour traffic. We have become much too impatient. If we text someone, and it takes them longer than 30 seconds to reply, we feel ignored or slighted.

Our insatiable need for instant gratification has made us dangerously more impatient. God-forbid we have to wait for anything. But some things just take time and are worth waiting for.

My friend Sharon, a talented graphic artist, told me that she calls our generation the "Before and After" Generation. She was specifically speaking about the fact that our generation is the last one to be alive both

259

before and after the Internet. So we should remember a time when we had to wait for things. How soon we forget.

Technology surely has not helped us to be more patient. I remember a time when, in order for you to get a photograph of your adorable baby sent to his grandmother, you had to take the photograph, wait until you used the entire roll up, usually 30 pictures, and then the roll of film was dropped off to be "developed." If the photo shop was "quick" at that time, the prints would be available in 3 or 4 days. Then you had to drive to the shop to pick them up and send the picture through the mail, which is now referred to as "snail mail."

By the time Grandma got the picture of her newborn grandson, he'd often be cutting teeth. (I miss printed photos.) Now my cousin Leslie can take a picture of his sleeping baby son Jakari in Miami, and text it to his mother Tillie in New York, all before the baby even wakes from his nap.

Patience – A Principle that Takes Practice

I was reminded about our need for patience all too much recently when trying to cook pot stickers. I love those dumpling type appetizers, but they truly got their name for a reason. I would go to the Asian market in town and buy them in the huge bags and freeze them. You're supposed to brown them on the flat side, and if done properly, they're not supposed to stick to the pan. But every time I made them, they ruined my pan because they would stick and fall apart, and I had to throw them out.

Since I loved them so much, I had to get to the bottom of how to get these pot stickers not to stick to my pan. Was it the oil? Was it that water? Did I cook them too long or not long enough? I had to find out. I checked in with some of my chef friends on what to do to solve this challenge in my life. Low and behold, I discovered the two things I was doing wrong.

First, I was moving the pot stickers around in the pan as they were cooking, probably in an effort to rush it along. That meant that I should have just left them alone, undisturbed, until the process was complete. Second, I was not willing to wait for them to do their thing on their own in the necessary amount of time it took to cook perfectly. Each time, I tried to cook them, I kept lifting them up and checking to see if what I was expecting to happen was actually happening. I had no pot sticker

faith.

Once I grew tired of wasting my money and time on burned, stuck-to-the-pan pot stickers, I decided to let Patience do her thing. Now I put the oil in the pan, place the pot stickers in, pour a little bit of water on top, cover the pan and walk away. I have faith in the process. Now, after only 8 minutes, I have perfect pot stickers that never stick to the pan. Who knew that Faith and Patience needed to be used even in the kitchen?

Let Patience Do Her Work
We live in a society today of instant everything. Patience is something that if you don't use it, you will most certainly lose it. Count it all as joy when you face challenges, knowing that the trying of your faith worketh patience and perseverance. Seems tough, right? But here's the good news. If you let Patience have her perfect work, you'll be perfect and entire wanting nothing. (See James 1:2-4.)

I gotta tell you, I really like that deal. So what we are being told to do is to see even our problems/adversity as pure joy. Once perseverance has had its time to work on us, we will be mature and complete, lacking nothing. Alright, count me in. I can do this because I really want to be lacking nothing. If I just have to have patience, and I'm guaranteed that it will come, then I'm good with that. I can find a way to be comfortable being temporarily uncomfortable if that is the only way I will move on. Especially since I know that trouble doesn't last always.

"No winter lasts forever; no spring skips its turn."
~ Hal Borland

Author William Feather once said that success is largely a matter of hanging on after others have let go. So when you think you've reached the end of your rope, tie a knot and hold on.

Besides, the patient path is often the fastest way. Some things just can't be rushed. Hang in there; Patience is doing her thing.

Final Thoughts

"If we could sell our experiences for what they cost us, we'd all be millionaires."
- Abigail Van Buren

What are you doing with this magnificent and precious life of yours? I pray you refuse to waste one more moment in frustration, worry, and doubt. By now you see that it is all B.S. anyhow. It's simply not what it looks like. You must change the way you are looking at things.

You must count it all joy. Everything. The good, the bad and the ugly. No matter what comes your way - count it all joy. The events and circumstances of your life are happening for you and not to you. When you count everything all joy, it removes adversity's sting. If you are willing to "see" it correctly, there is always a benefit, a silver-lining in which each of our problems are wrapped. It has to be. There is no other way. Besides, when you get through this, - and you surely will - you will be so much stronger and better than you ever were before.

You have been given the unique opportunity to rise higher in your consciousness. The state of mind that you are in now is not worthy of you. It's time to move. Accept the invitation. You have been chosen for this experience so you can come up a bit higher. Rise, take up your bed and walk.

"One sees great things from the valley; only small things from the peak."
- G.K. Chesterton

Stop performing CPR on dead problems. It is you who is breathing life into them. Change your mind. It's that simple.

Agree with all adversity. Don't fight it. Fight nothing and no one. For what you resist (or fight) persists. Stop it now. Your resistance to that unpleasant situation is the root of your suffering. Stop fighting people and problems.

I promise you, just like that raging river that I was fighting, that I thought was trying to consume me, was the same river that carried me gently to safety. But not until I listened to that still small voice that told

me to R-E-L-A-X. Only then was I able to be freed from fear and worry. It happens immediately. You are just a decision away.

Reject as real any problem or limitation you now think as so. If you are continually knocking on a door that is not opening for you, don't worry, it just may not be your door. Move on. Knock elsewhere but keep knocking. Never give up on your heart's desires. Be child-like in your asking but not childish.

> *"I tell you not to worry about your life."*
> - Matthew 6:25

Trouble don't last always. Your problem only lasts as long as it needs to. Count it all joy today. Psalm 30:5 tells us that weeping may endure for a night, but joy comes in the morning. Well, I've got news for you...It's morning.

We are usually frustrated because we are trying to get something we already have. You came fully equipped with everything you need for this journey. Those who trust in the Lord never lack a good thing (Psalm 34:10). So, you can rest assured that you have everything you need for the season you are in right now. If you don't have it right now, you don't need it right now.

> *"There is no path to peace. Peace is the path."*
> - Mahatma Gandhi

The greatest self-help book ever written puts in a nutshell why being a Frustrated Believer is a necessary step in your transcendence to a higher state of mind. In II Corinthians 12:9, God says, ..My power works best in weakness". So be glad. Challenges in this life are necessary. But suffering is optional.

> *"According to your Faith, be it unto you. "*
> - Matthew 9:29

Frustration is caused by our ignorance of who and what we are. We perish for lack of knowledge. Often it is simply a lack of wisdom. For when we know better, we do better. Go get wisdom. Wisdom is better than weapons of war. Pay whatever you have to get it. The investment is worth it. It will change your life, and you can pass it on to generations to come.

> *"Never begrudge the money you spend on your own education."*
> - Jim Rohn

But you must believe. Believe in the incredible power of the human mind - your human mind. There are more possibilities available to us in each moment than we even realize. But you must believe in miracles to experience miracles. All things are possible to those who are willing to believe.

Change the way you look at your life and everything in it. Examine your Belief Systems. (B.S.) It is through these systems that you process your world. Sometimes your Faith has to go through an upgrade. Let me upgrade you. My clients, often wrinkled by worry and frustration, come to me for a "Faith Lift".

Faith is your personal assistant. Put Faith to work for you. There is no mountain Faith cannot move, but not without what powers Faith, which is Love. Give love away like your life depends on it because it does. Since your Faith is powered by Love, if you are not walking in Love, your Faith will not work. Period.

> *"When Fear knocks at your door, let your personal assistant, Faith answer it. Then change the locks, so Fear doesn't try to break in again."*
> - Shelley Roxanne

By now you know that the Law of Attraction is not the only Secret. There are many. But if you don't apply them to your life, they remain secrets and thus ineffective for you. You are where you are in your life because you chose to be there. If you don't like where you are, choose to change.

People only change for one of two reasons. Either they desire something better so strongly that they want to change, or they hurt so

264

badly that they have to change. You can do this the hard way or you can do this the easy way. It's your choice. Don't be forced to change. Do it voluntarily. The way of the stubborn is so hard. Remember, when change is necessary, not to change is destruction.

"The unexamined life is not worth living."
- Socrates

The Kingdom of Heaven is within and is here now for the taking. There is a reservation reserved just for you. Go ahead and move in.

There is only one you, and you pass this way only once. Make the most of it. From this day forward, let the good times roll. Be silly. Be crazy. Be more. Demand that your life have tremendous joy and fun in it. Accept nothing less. For the very best is yet to come.

Life is a song worth singing...so, cue the music.
I love you.

About the Author

For the last 25 years, Shelley Roxanne has been on a mission. As a National Woman of Influence and the reigning Queen of Optimism, Shelley has emerged as someone who's actually lived the personal and professional principles she espouses. She really walks the talk. Shelley has delivered her innovative, unique and powerful life-changing principles to enthusiastic audiences around the globe through her various endeavors - Optimistic Radio, Optimistic University, Optimistic h20 and Optimistic Leadership Academy for Boys - to name a few. Internationally known as the "Architect of the Optimistic Lifestyle," Shelley Roxanne is a recognized leader and foremost expert in her field. As a highly skilled, dynamic speaker and sought after coach, she is frequently called upon by top executives, athletes, musicians and celebrities to bring her powerful, passionate and engaging style to their teams and organizations.

Shelley Roxanne is one of America's foremost authorities on developing the potential within an individual by coaching them on how to live a maximized life. As the Founder of Optimistic, Inc., a Personal and Professional Development Company, Shelley Roxanne brings a wealth of experience with years in the Corporate World where she left her indelible mark in the areas of Management Development/ Human Resources, Employee Relations, Diversity and Corporate Culture Initiatives, Marketing, and Public Relations. Often called "The Company Doctor," Shelley has been a principal architect of many successful organizational change efforts.

Her newly released best-selling book, *The Frustrated Believer: What to Do When You Don't Know What to Do*, is already being considered today's new self-help standard. The ground-breaking book is a fun, provocative and profoundly insightful read that illustrates how anyone - no matter what their, age, faith, religion or personal philosophy - can enjoy this exciting journey called life.

The Frustrated Believer illustrates how changing the way you look at things can change what you are experiencing in a positive, meaningful

way. The book is full of engaging personal accounts intertwined with substantial cutting-edge strategies for your successful journey that is backed up by 50 years of exhaustive, comprehensive research.

Critics overwhelmingly agree Shelley is unlike anyone you've ever met before. According to Steven Silbiger, Author of *The Jewish Phenomenon*, Shelley is "one of those special people who cause a movement to begin". This movement of Optimism has been convincing even the most pessimistic types that "The Best Is Yet To Come".

Shelley's philanthropic efforts are equally as impressive. In 2007, she founded The Optimistic Leadership Academy for Boys. An Academy for boys who's mission is to inspire excellence in our sons while offering activities that help these wonderful boys realize their potential and teach them to reach further than they ever imagined possible. It has been said that greatness in life is not measured by what you do...but by what you inspire others to do. If that is true, then Shelley Roxanne is quickly approaching legendary status.

To find out more about Shelley and her many endeavors or to bring Shelley to your next event, visit

www.shelleyroxanne.com
Twitter: @SheRoxTV
Facebook: facebook.com/shelleyroxanne

267

CPSIA information can be obtained
at www.ICGtesting.com
Printed in the USA
FSOW01n1037180117
29776FS